Palgrave Critical Studies in Post-Conflict Recovery

Series Editors
Sultan Barakat
Department of Politics
University of York
York, UK

Sansom Milton
Post-war Reconstruction and Development
University of York
York, UK

This series seeks to advance original research in the broadly defined area of post-conflict recovery. The Pivot format of the series is designed to meet the growing need for the provision of *timely*, *focused*, *theoretically-rigorous*, and *applied* research into conflict-affected environments. The aim is to bridge the theory and practice of post-conflict recovery across a range of disciplinary approaches and interventionary logics including but not limited to humanitarian action, conflict resolution, post-war reconstruction, peacebuilding, state-building, and transitional justice. It welcomes submissions from researchers, practitioners and policy makers, in particular from the Global South.

More information about this series at
http://www.palgrave.com/gp/series/14708

Daniel Serwer

From War to Peace in the Balkans, the Middle East and Ukraine

Daniel Serwer
School of Advanced International
   Studies
Johns Hopkins University
Washington, DC, USA

Palgrave Critical Studies in Post-Conflict Recovery
ISBN 978-3-030-02172-6   ISBN 978-3-030-02173-3 (eBook)
https://doi.org/10.1007/978-3-030-02173-3

Library of Congress Control Number: 2018957680

© The Editor(s) (if applicable) and The Author(s) 2019. This book is an open access publication.
Open Access This book is licensed under the terms of the Creative Commons Attribution 4.0 International License (http://creativecommons.org/licenses/by/4.0/), which permits use, sharing, adaptation, distribution and reproduction in any medium or format, as long as you give appropriate credit to the original author(s) and the source, provide a link to the Creative Commons license and indicate if changes were made.
The images or other third party material in this book are included in the book's Creative Commons license, unless indicated otherwise in a credit line to the material. If material is not included in the book's Creative Commons license and your intended use is not permitted by statutory regulation or exceeds the permitted use, you will need to obtain permission directly from the copyright holder.
The use of general descriptive names, registered names, trademarks, service marks, etc. in this publication does not imply, even in the absence of a specific statement, that such names are exempt from the relevant protective laws and regulations and therefore free for general use.
The publisher, the authors, and the editors are safe to assume that the advice and information in this book are believed to be true and accurate at the date of publication. Neither the publisher nor the authors or the editors give a warranty, express or implied, with respect to the material contained herein or for any errors or omissions that may have been made. The publisher remains neutral with regard to jurisdictional claims in published maps and institutional affiliations.

Cover illustration: Pattern adapted from an Indian cotton print produced in the 19th century

This Palgrave Pivot imprint is published by the registered company Springer Nature Switzerland AG
The registered company address is: Gewerbestrasse 11, 6330 Cham, Switzerland

Fig. 1 Kiepert, Heinrich. Generalkarte des Turkischen Kriegsschauplatzes: auf Grund der Carte Generale des Provinces Europeennes et Asiatiques de L'Empire Ottoman. (Berlin: Heinrich Kiepert, 1916) Map. https://www.loc.gov/item/2013593013/

Fig. 2 Twenty-first century Balkans, Middle East and Ukraine

To the people of the Balkans, who have suffered and deserve better

Preface

This book aims to analyze the wars of Yugoslav succession after 1989 and subsequent peacebuilding of the 1990s and 2000s, up to the present. I know of no comparable effort. When a group of Fulbright scholars heading for the Balkans asked in the summer of 2014 for a book that gave an overview of the recent history, I was stumped. There is no single book to recommend about the conflicted parts of the region and their recovery from war, though there are good books focused on the dissolution of former Yugoslavia and the postwar trajectories of individual countries. This thin volume is a belated answer to the Fulbrighters' request for an accessible treatment that treats the whole region's recent wars and subsequent peace.

The book began with lectures on Bosnia (I follow the usual American practice of shortening "Bosnia and Herzegovina"), Macedonia, Kosovo, Serbia, and the Balkans region as a part of Europe. I've added an introduction on "Why the Balkans?" and a concluding chapter on the implications for the Middle East and Ukraine, as people often try to apply lessons from the Balkans to those areas, which lie close by and share some history in the Ottoman empire. I have spent most of the last 15 years working on Iraq, Syria, Libya, Egypt, and other majority Arab countries suffering from conflict and experiencing often unsuccessful transitions from autocracy. I understand those who see in the ongoing tragedies in Ukraine and Syria multiple reflections of the 1990s conflicts, especially in Bosnia and Kosovo. But valid conclusions require we understand what is specific to the context and what is more generally applicable.

My emphasis is on explanation and re-interpretation, an exegesis of events that in retrospect have clearer significance than when they happened. I have tried to rely on the best, though mainly secondary, sources. I have also had access to some declassified State Department cables, released under the Freedom of Information Act. The most relevant ones I've included in the footnotes. My personal experiences inform many of the events and my interpretation of them.

For almost 25 years the people of the Balkans have tried to keep me abreast of developments, explain their issues, make me understand their plight and hopes, and suggest remedies. Unlike many of them, I believe the region has made enormous progress, even if problems that could threaten regional peace and security remain, especially in Kosovo and Serbia as well as in Bosnia. As its people approach resolution of the last remaining major conflict issues in their region, they merit wholehearted support and encouragement to consolidate peace and democracy by completing the process of joining Euro-Atlantic institutions, with all the manifold requirements that entails. This book is intended as a contribution to their efforts.

Washington, USA   Daniel Serwer

Acknowledgements

Credit is due to many. Purdue University Professor Charles Ingrao, whose Scholarly Initiative I encouraged, appears in this book in the footnotes referencing its *Confronting the Yugoslav Controversies*. I am grateful to all its European and American contributors of varied origins and ethnicities for their courage and commitment in trying to sort things out in a way true to their diverse perspectives. Clemson University Professor Vladimir Matić, who had the decency to resign from the Yugoslav Foreign Ministry before the worst Milošević abuses were perpetrated, read an early draft and offered perspicacious comments as well as encouragement to complete this book.

Rrap Kryeziu, a Kosovar American and then a rising senior at my alma mater Haverford, worked with me in the summer of 2015 and again in 2018 to check the facts, challenge interpretations, and straighten out footnotes, formatting, and other annoying details. Marko Grujičić, a Serbian student at the Johns Hopkins School of Advanced International Studies (SAIS), likewise helped in academic year 2015/16. Martin Naunov, a Macedonian American and rising senior at Middlebury College, joined the effort in the summer of 2016. SAIS Professor Siniša Vuković, a Montenegrin, read and commented on the penultimate draft, to excellent effect. Copyeditor Jonathan Lawrence whipped the final version into shape.

I owe the time and intellectual as well as administrative and library support needed to the Johns Hopkins School of Advanced International Studies and its Conflict Management program, personified by

Administrative Coordinator Isabelle Talpain-Long as well as my predecessors as its Director, Professors P. Terrence Hopmann and I. William Zartman. I feel deep gratitude to each of them.

Praise for *From War to Peace in the Balkans, the Middle East and Ukraine*

"Dan Serwer was there at the start of international interventions in the Balkans. He is a clear-eyed observer of what has worked and what has not in a region still at peace but still troubled. Dan has earned his observations from decades in the field, and this book is well worth reading."
—Madeleine K. Albright, *Former US Secretary of State, USA*

"Daniel Serwer, who has worked in and on the Balkans for decades, has produced a fine book on the collapse of the region after Tito. Focused heavily on Bosnia and Kosovo, he catalogues the successes and failures in US and European policy in the region. Hard-hitting, his heroes have their blemishes showing; his scoundrels are far from being caricatured. For aficionados and those seeking an excellent narrative with informed comment this is an important read."
—Thomas R. Pickering, *Former US Under Secretary of State for Political Affairs and Ambassador to the UN and Russia, USA*

"This is a long overdue study and I can think of no-one better to write it than Dan Serwer. He was actively involved in the Balkan troubles of recent years as a policy maker and shaper of events, right from the start, gaining a widespread reputation for his judgement and wisdom. This is a cool, rational, and expert lesson of what we should learn from this period and how it is relevant to the challenges we face today."
—Lord Paddy Ashdown, *Former High Representative in Bosnia and Herzegovina (2002–2006), UK*

"After a quarter of a century of engagement by the international community in the Western Balkans, a region marred by crisis and acute conflict in the wake of the dissolution of Yugoslavia, much progress has been made, but more attention and engagement are still required. Daniel Serwer, a prominent scholar and a key actor in efforts to promote peace in the region, helps us to understand the historical background, complexities of the regional environment and impact of political initiatives. While each conflict has its own dynamics, many lessons that are painfully learned are too quickly forgotten. This book reminds us of the successes and failures of international engagement in the former Yugoslavia. We should keep these in mind when addressing outstanding issues in the region or attempting to resolve other complex conflicts with a direct or indirect impact on European security."

—Lamberto Zannier, *Special Representative of the UN Secretary General for Kosovo, 2008–2011, Secretary General of the Organisation for Security and Cooperation in Europe (2011–2017), and OSCE High Commissioner for Minorities (2017–present), the Netherlands*

Contents

1 Introduction — 1

2 Why the Balkans? — 13

3 Bosnia: Prelude, Disease, and Sequelae — 29

4 Macedonia: Timely Prevention Works — 53

5 Kosovo and Serbia: Loveless Marriage, Difficult Divorce — 71

6 Can the Balkans Join the West? — 91

7 What Should the Middle East and Ukraine Learn from the Balkans? — 115

Selected Bibliography — 137

Index — 141

CHAPTER 1

Introduction

Abstract Why and how the Balkans came apart, and what the United States, Europe, the United Nations, and other international organizations did to put the region back together, is too important to be ignored. Doubts about the virtue of what was done abound, but the region is demonstrably in better shape today than it was in the 1990s. Understanding the Balkans can inform what we do elsewhere and help the region understand its own history, with a view to avoiding a future implosion. The Dayton agreements ended the war in Bosnia in 1995, the Kosovo War ended in 1999, and the armed conflict in Macedonia ended in 2001. It is time to take stock.

Keywords Balkans · EU · NATO · Intervention · International guarantees

The Balkans are on no one's list of priority areas to study these days. Nothing I say here will change that, but the difficult process, serious barriers, and relatively positive outcomes of international peace- and state-building interventions in the Balkans can shed light on challenges we face in other parts of the world and suggest ways to deal with them. The extraordinarily costly, highly militarized, and miserably unhappy, if not yet quite failed, interventions in Iraq and Afghanistan should not be the only ones that inform thinking about how to go about enabling people in conflicted societies to secure, govern, and prosper themselves. Nor should setbacks in the Balkans since 2008, after serious progress in the previous decade, make us abandon hope that the region can remain at peace. In an era when security gaps, governance failures, creeping autocracy, and social and economic exclusion are creating fertile ground for extremism, it behooves us to contemplate what has been achieved in the Balkans, even if the outcomes are less salubrious than many of us would like.

It is troubling that much of the Balkans story is forgotten, or mistakenly remembered as the outcome of deeply ingrained and seemingly interminable ancient hatreds. Many otherwise well-informed people know little or nothing about the wars that accompanied the dissolution of Socialist Yugoslavia, unless they are among the relatively few who have served there. They are puzzled why the United States intervened militarily in Bosnia and Kosovo. News headlines from the Balkans that focus on tales of woe discourage deeper inquiry. My colleagues at the State Department, in European foreign ministries, and in academia on both continents doubt much has been achieved. Some even deem the 1990s interventions a miserable failure. They rightly complain about corruption and abuse of power, state capture, autocratic tendencies, lack of accountability for war crimes and human rights abuses, persistent ethnic tensions, youth unemployment, lagging economic growth, growing extremism, and constraints on freedom of the press. All those ills plague the Balkans today.

But these complaints are an indication of progress, not failure. The ills were no less present during the most recent Balkan wars, but few complained about them when mass murder and genocide were ongoing. Today's reality in the Balkans is unsatisfying and the failures frustrating, but the outcomes so far are demonstrable improvements over the past. Although many people from the region will tell you that things were better under Tito, that reflects their appreciation of him for the recovery from World War II and palpable disappointments from the 1990s, not today's objective reality. Serious problems remain, but prospects for all the countries of the region eventually to meet the increasingly strenuous requirements to enter the European Union, and NATO if they like, are decent, provided they continue on the path of political and economic reform.

Other observers question whether the EU will be ready and able to receive the Balkan states who are not yet members even if they do qualify for membership. The enlargement process has been frozen since Croatia's 2013 accession. The successful Brexit referendum in June 2016 and growing nationalist sentiment in Hungary, Poland, France, Denmark, the Netherlands, Italy, and other European countries threaten to make it impossible for the EU to continue to enlarge, as each prospective member will need its accession treaty ratified in all member states. Despite a European Commission commitment to unfreeze enlargement in 2025, on many days it appears Europe is becoming less democratic and more Balkan, rather than the Balkans more democratic and more European.

NATO is also in a period of introspection and doubt. It faces a serious Russian challenge in Ukraine and a growing one in the Baltics, both of which raise questions about whether the Alliance can defend even its current members, never mind new ones in the Balkans who will be able to contribute only marginally to NATO's defense. Donald Trump, elected president in November 2016, has expressed doubts about the value of the Alliance to the United States, an interest in partnering with Russia, and an intention of making security guarantees available only to countries whose military expenditures meet the NATO goal of 2% of GDP. Prospective members will face tough questions about what they are able and willing to contribute to the Alliance. No one can predict when, or if, wider Balkans membership in NATO will become possible, although the 2017 accession of Montenegro and Macedonia's 2018 invitation to join suggest that the door is not closed tight.

Still others doubt that the 1990s interventions did any good, forgetting what would have happened had they not occurred. It is not plausible that things would have been better had NATO not intervened at all, leaving Balkan leaders to their own all-too-often homicidal devices. They had already killed about one hundred thousand people in Bosnia by the time of the NATO intervention there. Close to another ten thousand died later in Kosovo. It is easy to imagine how things might have deteriorated without intervention. Today's concerns about recruitment of foreign fighters in the Balkans to go to Syria and Iraq would be far greater if Bosnia had been partitioned, leaving a non-viable and resentful rump Islamic state at its center, or if some part of Kosovo had been allowed to merge with Albania or the Albanian-populated part of Macedonia. Those precedents for ethnic partition would have destroyed the international norm against redrawing borders to accommodate ethnic differences, making a situation like the one we face in Ukraine far more difficult to manage than it is today, when at least the norm is clear if not the means of getting Russia to respect it. The results of intervention in the Balkans may be ugly, but the results of non-intervention would have been uglier.

Even those who accept that proposition will not always agree with my interpretation of events. What I say here about the Dayton peace negotiations, which I interpret not as a triumph of American diplomacy backed by force but rather as Milošević snatching what he could from near certain defeat, will be controversial. Some will take offense at my view that the Macedonia "name" issue has its origins in well-founded insecurity about Greek identity rather than irredentist territorial ambitions on the part of Slavs with no right to be called "Macedonian." Others may find me soft on Kosovo, which I consider a relative success in post–Cold War state-building, even if its sovereignty is still incomplete. Or they may object to my enthusiasm for the nonviolent protests that led to the fall of Milošević and initiated a democratic transition, also still not completed, in Serbia.

None of these are views I would have held in the form presented here as an American diplomat in the decade after the Berlin Wall fell. Time offers perspective, but interpretation in the Balkans presents enormous challenges. Memory can both hinder and advance understanding. Ethnic nationalists keep alive only the memory of what was done to their own kind and celebrate the victories of their own ethnic heroes. People whose parents were once citizens of the same country no longer have a shared sense of history, culture, or destiny. Despite the cultural similarities in language, music, and cuisine, nationalist Balkan leaders in the 1990s underlined mainly differences, in an effort to generate distinctions that would support their political perspectives and career prospects. Young Kosovars do not recognize the Serbian language, which a generation earlier their parents spoke fluently. Conflicts are too often preserved. Far less attention is paid to mutual dependency, common culture, or once prevalent feelings of solidarity.

The disintegration of Socialist Yugoslavia got quick and capable scholarly attention.[1] Susan Woodward identified state weakness as the main cause, induced in part by economic failure, the collapse of a bipolar world in which Socialist Yugoslavia had found a unique niche, and the stress caused by the international community's insistence on liberal economic and political reform. While not denying Serbian aggression and ethnic nationalism, she treated them more as consequences than causes.[2] Misha Glenny likewise traced the roots of what he termed the Third Balkan War to a weak Socialist Yugoslavia, albeit with more emphasis on ethnic differences. Nationalist leaders, he demonstrated, succeeded in mobilizing popular fears to their respective causes.[3] Journalists Allan Little and Laura Silber wove a captivating narrative captured also in film, with more emphasis on Serbian nationalism and aggression.[4] More recently, Catherine Baker treats the 1990s wars as resulting from the interaction among opportunistic nationalist leaders who mobilized ethnic differences to compete for power within the context of a weak Yugoslav state, destroying it in the process.[5] Josip Glaurdić emphasizes the way European and American "realist" hesitancy to intervene enabled Balkan leadership's worst inclinations.[6] Eric Gordy believes scholarship has been excessively focused on a top-down view of states and political elites, without enough attention to the societies and people of former Yugoslavia as well as their interaction with the newly emerging states.[7]

Each of these approaches has merits. My own understanding corresponds to the canonical levels of analysis: individuals, domestic factors, and international factors.[8] Milošević's ambitions and capabilities, the ideological and practical implications of territorial ethnic nationalism he provoked within each of the Yugoslav successor states, and the breakup of former Yugoslavia combined to produce an astounding array of interlinked interstate and intrastate conflicts. With the Yugoslav state and its Marxist foundations collapsing in the aftermath of the Cold War, ethnic nationalists sought to gain and maintain power by promising to protect their respective ethnic groups, each of which felt threatened. Most were unable to do much harm on their own. But one Balkan leader, Slobodan Milošević, had the political will and military means to do more than the others. The Greater Serbia project he adopted became the main proximate cause of the Balkan wars of the 1990s, as nationalist leaders of other ethnic groups reacted to the threat he posed.[9] This was the ethnic version of a security dilemma: what the Serbs did to protect themselves made others feel less secure, creating a vicious spiral that resulted in civil wars in Slovenia, Croatia, Bosnia, and Kosovo. Call it a post–Cold War domino theory if you like. The United States and Europe failed initially to invest the resources necessary to prevent war, but they eventually intervened to good effect with both military and civilian means to end the conflicts and build peace.

While Slovenia won its war, the other domino wars of Yugoslav succession ended in negotiated agreements: Croatia (the Erdut Agreement in 1995), Bosnia (the Washington Agreement of 1994 as well as the Dayton Accords of 1995), Kosovo (UN Security Council Resolution 1244 in 1999), and Macedonia (the Ohrid Agreement of 2001). All these resulted in part from international pressures, sometimes military and sometimes diplomatic and political, with economic relief and benefits thrown in for good measure. In conflict-management terms, the United States and Europe, working in tandem, "ripened" these situations in order to produce the kind of "mutually hurting stalemates" regarded as necessary for negotiated settlements.[10] The willingness of the Americans and Europeans to guarantee peace, while leaving in place many of the wartime leaders, made negotiated arrangements enticing that would otherwise surely have been rejected. This is consistent with Barbara Walter's scholarly work, which emphasizes the importance of promised international guarantees to negotiation processes.[11]

But negotiated settlements are compromises that do not necessarily remove the drivers of conflict. In the Balkans they allowed both warring parties and their ideas to survive, at least in the political realm. Women, who played almost no role in taking the region to war, played little more in shaping its aftermath.[12] Statistically speaking, the exclusion of women makes peaceful, democratic outcomes less likely.[13] The postwar transitions in the Balkans were managed almost entirely by men without high-level purges (except for those indicted for crimes committed during wartime), people-to-people reconciliation efforts, and the kind of sustained dialogue within and between civil society actors that scholars and practitioners think vital.[14] United Nations, European Union, and American administrators and diplomats as well as peacekeeping troops from many countries played vital roles in stabilization and reconstruction, but they also committed crimes, sometimes allegedly on a grand financial scale. Transparency and accountability were lacking. The example the internationals set was not always a salubrious one: instances of corruption and sexual misconduct cast a broad shadow. More than one American ambassador in the region resigned under that cloud.

The construction of new political orders was highly conflictual. Studies of them have been fragmented, reflecting the situation in the region.[15] Studies elsewhere have identified two main factors affecting peace implementation: resources, including political will as well as troops and finances, and the difficulty of the environment.[16] The Balkan peace processes have not lacked resources. It is even arguable that Bosnia eventually suffered from too much international commitment, and Kosovo was a luxury peace implementation mission almost from the first. The environment in the Balkans was difficult because of both neighboring countries and local elites, which are known to be decisive factors.[17] The postwar international peace missions in Bosnia, Kosovo, and Macedonia were at least partly successful because they provided vital international guarantees of peace implementation and blocked violent moves supported from neighbors (from Croatia in Bosnia, from Serbia in Kosovo, and from Kosovo in Macedonia) as well as demilitarizing and co-opting local elites. The Balkans generally lack a third environmental factor known to be detrimental to peace-building in other contexts: readily tradable commodities like oil or minerals that can support resistance to peace implementation, though some might argue that trafficking in cigarettes, drugs, and people has played an analogous role.

The international agreements and other commitments that brought peace to the region were all based on the principle that preexisting borders should not be moved to accommodate ethnic differences. Yugoslavia did not just disintegrate. It fell apart into its component federal units, namely, the republics that had constituted Socialist Yugoslavia, as recommended by the Badinter Commission to the European Community in 1991.[18] Since the borders of those federal units did not correspond to ethnic identities, this meant each republic faced issues with ethnic groups that did not constitute a numerical majority. The main non-majority ethnic groups included Serbs in Slovenia and Croatia, Serbs and Croats in Bosnia and Herzegovina, Albanians in Serbia and Macedonia, and Bosniaks as well as Albanians and Serbs in Montenegro. Much of the history of the wars and the subsequent peace revolves around the interactions among these groups within each post-Yugoslav state and between adjacent states.

Ethnic identity in the Balkans is defined today along both religious and linguistic lines. Apart from the atheists in the region, some of whom still identify themselves as Yugoslavs (South Slavs), Serbs usually identify as Orthodox Christians, Croats as Catholics, and Bosniaks as Muslims. But theology has nothing to do with their contemporary conflicts. You can forget about the *Filioque* (an arcane but historically important dispute on the relationship among the Father, the Son, and the Holy Ghost) and the resulting Great Schism that split the Roman Catholic Church from the Eastern Orthodox in the Middle Ages. The number of ministerial posts and jobs in state-owned industries is today far more important to people who claim to be defending their cherished religious identities and heritages.

Albanians are mostly Muslim in religious affiliation, if they have any (especially in Kosovo, many do not). They define themselves linguistically: an Albanian is someone who speaks Albanian (or whose parents spoke Albanian), an Indo-European language with little in common with the Slavic languages today identified as Bosnian, Croatian, Serbian, Montenegrin, Slovenian, and Macedonian. The first four, known until the wars of Yugoslav succession as Serbo-Croatian, are mutually comprehensible. The distinctions among the dialects were originally geographical, but today ethnic nationalists claim they are distinct languages. Macedonian and Slovenian are Slavic languages more difficult for Serbo-Croatian speakers to understand, though many do.

Balkan Muslims, both Bosniak (the non-religious term often favored by Slavic Muslims, whether they live in Bosnia or not) and Albanian, owe their existence to the Ottoman Empire, which dominated the southern part of the region for more than 450 years, from the conquest of Constantinople (today's Istanbul) in 1453 until World War I. The Ottomans governed their empire without homogenizing its population. Non-Muslims were second-class citizens not usually permitted to hold administrative or military power, but so long as they paid their taxes and did not challenge the Ottomans militarily or politically, they could exercise some degree of autonomy within a distinct "national" community (*millet*), especially concerning personal status issues like marriage, divorce, and inheritance. Otherwise, governance was administered by patriarchal warlords whose power depended on plunder rather than productive economic activity.[19] Consent of the governed was enforced with violence.

The *millet* practice is the root of the idea that ethnic groups have rights to govern themselves and not be forced to do things that other ethnic groups want them to do, even if the decision is taken by a numerical majority. Numerical majorities only count within ethnic groups, not between them. This concept of group rights survived the end of the Ottoman Empire, became a foundational idea in monarchical as well as Socialist Yugoslavia, and remains an issue throughout the Balkans, as well as the Middle East. Ottoman culture and language are by no means limited to Muslims. Their traces are found in majority-Catholic Croatia as well as in majority-Orthodox Serbia, even if it will not always be appreciated if you say so.

Group rights differ from individual rights. The U.S. Constitution starts with the words "We the People." It protects (especially in its first ten amendments) individual rights. Balkan constitutions often enumerate "constituent" peoples, those groups that have the privilege and responsibility of forming the state. It is as if they start "We the Peoples." That small difference is a big one. If you are not enumerated, your group will not have the same status or political role as the groups that are. If you are listed, you are not considered a "minority," no matter how small your numbers. In most of Europe, rights of groups, not just individuals, to culture, education, religion, and language are explicitly recognized. Only France has refused to sign the European Framework Convention on Protection of National Minorities, which includes group rights (albeit for numerical minorities) that are not recognized there or in the United States.

In addition to the Ottoman legacy of group rights, there is one other historical episode that bears on events since 1989. World War II and its aftermath in the Balkans is still remembered, though not always accurately, including atrocities committed against many individuals and ethnic groups.[20] Croats and Serbs still dispute how many of each group the (World War II fascist) Independent State of Croatia killed in the concentration camp at Jasenovac. The conflict within the Yugoslav resistance between Communist partisans led by Tito and monarchist "chetniks" led by Draža Mihailović, who were more devoted to creation of a Greater Serbia than to defeating the fascists, was also ferocious, especially at the end of the war. Many Serb nationalists are still unabashed admirers of the chetniks, whom they regard as worthy predecessors.

This Communist/anti-Communist split has survived the end of Communism in much of the Balkans. In the 1990s, most Croatian attitudes toward World War II were equivocal, but among the extreme nationalists, including among the Bosnian Croats, the fascist pedigree was a source of pride. It was on prominent display after Croatia in July 2018 managed to finish second in the World Cup. The historical connection between modern-day Croatian nationalism and World War II fascism is in any event often assumed by non-Croats and much resented by those who associate themselves with the Communist partisans. In 1995, the mayor of a central Bosnian town justified his resistance to letting Croats return who had been ethnically cleansed by the Bosniaks during the war by producing a photo of his former neighbors dressed in fascist uniforms and giving the straight-armed salute. "These are the people you want me to welcome back?" he asked rhetorically.

The split between people who trace their lineage to the Communists and those who trace it to anti-Communist nationalists is apparent not only in Serbia and Croatia but also in Macedonia, Bosnia, and Montenegro.

To outsiders, it is surprising, and disturbing, that even today this split is so palpable. Americans may have forgotten who was a Communist, or not care any longer, but people in the Balkans have not. This is especially true in Albania, where some of today's Socialists (presumed former Communists) and Democrats (presumed former anti-Communists) loathe each other with a passion usually associated with ethnic distinctions, not political ones. That ethnically indistinguishable Albanians can hate each other as much as Bosniaks and Serbs, or Serbs and Albanians, suggests that ethnic divisions are not the root of the problem.

The distribution of political power is. After explaining why the Balkan conflicts became so important in the 1990s and are again worthy of our attention now (Chapter 2), my narrative begins in still-ailing Bosnia and Herzegovina, with its war's prelude, disease, and sequelae (Chapter 3). We consider there why a decade of postwar progress has given way to more than a decade of stagnation and even backsliding. Next comes Macedonia, where international prevention under the UN flag proved better than a cure (Chapter 4), even if war was not completely avoided and difficult issues persist. There is now hope for major progress that would put Macedonia on a quick road to NATO and EU accession. In Serbia and Kosovo (Chapter 5), "divide and govern" became the necessary and still not quite complete outcome. They need to normalize their relations so that both countries can continue to progress. Montenegro and Albania, which remained mostly at peace with their neighbors (even during the near collapse of state authority in the latter), get short shrift in these chapters, but they make important cameo appearances, along with relatively peaceful Romania and Bulgaria, in the discussion of whether the Balkans can become part of the West (Chapter 6). My story ends in Ukraine and the Middle East (Chapter 7), much of which shares with the Balkans a past in the Ottoman Empire, a present plagued by war, and an uncertain future. Something analogous might be said of parts of Ukraine, which endured a similar relationship with the Russian Empire and faces some similar problems, but without the overlapping, multi-sided complexity of the Balkans and the Middle East.

Notes

1. For a masterful survey of the issues raised in the relevant academic literature up to 2005, see Sabrina P. Ramet, *Thinking About Yugoslavia: Scholarly Debates About the Yugoslav Breakup and the Wars in Bosnia and Kosovo* (New York: Cambridge University Press, 2009).

2. Susan L. Woodward, *Balkan Tragedy: Chaos and Dissolution After the Cold War* (Washington, DC: Brookings Institution, 1997).
3. Misha Glenny, *The Fall of Yugoslavia: The Third Balkan War* (London: Penguin Books, 1996).
4. Laura Silber and Allan Little, *The Death of Yugoslavia* (London: Penguin Books, 2010). Also see Vittorio Vida, "The Death of Yugoslavia." BBC Complete Documentary, YouTube video, 4:54:30, posted September 2012, https://www.youtube.com/watch?v=oODjsdLoSYo.
5. Catherine Baker, *The Yugoslav Wars of the 1990s* (Basingstoke: Palgrave Macmillan, 2015).
6. Josip Glaurdić, *The Hour of Europe: Western Powers and the Breakup of Yugoslavia* (New Haven: Yale University Press, 2011).
7. Eric Gordy, "On the Current and Future Research Agenda for Southeast Europe," in *Debating the End of Yugoslavia*, ed. Florian Bieber, Armina Galijaš, and Rory Archer (Burlington, VT: Ashgate, 2014), 11–22.
8. Jack S. Levy, "International Sources of Interstate and Intrastate War," in *Leashing the Dogs of War: Conflict Management in a Divided World*, ed. Chester A. Crocker, Fen Osler Hampson, and Pamela Aall (Washington, DC: USIP, 2008), 17–38.
9. James Gow, *The Serbian Project and Its Adversaries: A Strategy of War Crimes* (Montreal: McGill-Queen's University Press, 2003).
10. William Zartman, "Ripeness: The Hurting Stalemate and Beyond," in *International Conflict Resolution After the Cold War*, ed. Paul C. Stern and Daniel Druckman (Washington, DC: National Academy Press, 2000), 225–249, https://www.nap.edu/read/9897/chapter/7.
11. Barbara Walter, *Committing to Peace: The Successful Settlement of Civil Wars* (Princeton: Princeton University Press, 2002).
12. Swanee Hunt, *This Was Not Our War: Bosnian Women Reclaiming the Peace* (Durham: Duke University Press, 2004).
13. Valerie M. Hudson, Bonnie Ballif-Spanvill, Mary Caprioli, and Chad F. Emmett, *Sex and World Peace* (New York: Columbia University Press, 2014).
14. Harold H. Saunders, *Sustained Dialogue in Conflicts: Transformation and Change* (New York: Palgrave Macmillan, 2011).
15. Richard Caplan does, however, include the early Croatia, Bosnia, and Kosovo experiences (as well as East Timor) in his comparative study, *International Governance of War-Torn Territories: Rule and Reconstruction* (Oxford: Oxford University Press, 2008).
16. Stephen John Stedman, Donald Rothchild, and Elizabeth M. Cousens, eds., *Ending Civil Wars: The Implementation of Peace Agreements* (Boulder: Lynne Rienner, 2002).
17. James Dobbins, Laurel E. Miller, Stephanie Pezard, Christopher S. Chivvis, Julie E. Taylor, Keith Crane, Calin Trenkov-Wermuth, and

Tewodaj Mengistu, *Overcoming Obstacles to Peace: Local Factors in Nation-Building* (Santa Monica, CA: RAND Corporation, 2013), https://www.rand.org/pubs/research_reports/RR167.html.
18. Maurizio Ragazzi, "Conference on Yugoslavia Arbitration Commission: Opinions on Questions Arising from the Dissolution of Yugoslavia," *International Legal Materials* 31, no. 6 (November 1992): 1488–1526, https://www.jstor.org/stable/20693759.
19. Jasmin Mujanovic, *Hunger and Fury: The Crisis of Democracy in the Balkans* (Oxford: Oxford University Press, 2018), 22.
20. For a sampling see John Connelly, "Language and Blood," *Nation*, September 29, 2014, https://www.thenation.com/article/language-and-blood/.

Open Access This chapter is distributed under the terms of the Creative Commons Attribution 4.0 International License (http://creativecommons.org/licenses/by/4.0/), which permits use, duplication, adaptation, distribution and reproduction in any medium or format, as long as you give appropriate credit to the original author(s) and the source, a link is provided to the Creative Commons license and any changes made are indicated.

The images or other third party material in this chapter are included in the work's Creative Commons license, unless indicated otherwise in the credit line; if such material is not included in the work's Creative Commons license and the respective action is not permitted by statutory regulation, users will need to obtain permission from the license holder to duplicate, adapt or reproduce the material.

CHAPTER 2

Why the Balkans?

Abstract After trying to ignore the Balkans after the Cold War, the United States led NATO military interventions there at the height of the unipolar moment in 1995 (Bosnia) and 1999 (Kosovo) to stop wars that Washington feared would taint the post-Cold War world. Those interventions and a diplomatic one in Macedonia in 2001 were relatively successful, because they included serious international guarantees as well as major, multilateral, postwar peace- and state-building undertaken jointly by the United States and Europe with the consent of the warring parties. That experience suggests what will be necessary to deal with ongoing conflicts in Ukraine and the Middle East, though the multiplicity of players will make the latter far more difficult than the former.

Keywords Unipolar moment · CNN effect · Ethnic nationalism · State-building

In 2018 the United States and Europe worry about Iranian and North Korean nuclear weapons, Islamic State and Al Qaeda extremists, China's rise, Russian threats to elections as well as to Ukraine, and the war in Syria, which has inundated its neighbors and beyond with refugees. Europe is also preoccupied with its own economic and financial woes (a lengthy recession, a shaky euro, almost bankrupt Greece, and Brexit) as well as refugees and migrants, some still coming from the Balkans but

© The Author(s) 2019
D. Serwer, *From War to Peace in the Balkans, the Middle East and Ukraine*, Palgrave Critical Studies in Post-Conflict Recovery, https://doi.org/10.1007/978-3-030-02173-3_2

many more from the Middle East and North Africa, in part through the Balkans. Washington frets about Chinese economic competition and its growing security threat in the Asia Pacific, countering violent extremism as well as its own illegal immigrants. The Balkans did not appear for years on the Council on Foreign Relations list of thirty possible contingencies possibly requiring American attention, though it made the cut for 2018.[1] It might appear on a comparable European list, but not near the top.

It was not always so. In the 1990s the United States led dramatic international interventions to end the most recent Balkan wars, now largely forgotten. First in Bosnia in 1995 and then in Kosovo in 1999, American-led NATO forces bombed Serb forces, bringing Milošević to the negotiating table at Dayton and forcing him to retreat from Kosovo. The Balkans was then a major focus of American foreign policy. After the Soviet Union dissolved and the United States led a coalition to expel Iraq from Kuwait, the region absorbed endless hours of high-level energy and time.[2] Neither the 1994 genocide in Rwanda nor the 1996 Taliban takeover of Afghanistan attracted more attention in Washington. Both attracted less response.

American military intervention came on the heels of four years of European and United Nations failure to manage the Balkan conflicts successfully. For Europe, the dissolution of former Yugoslavia was an unwanted but unavoidable challenge: the Balkan wars threw refugees onto its doorstep and threatened to destabilize the immediate neighborhood. The European Community (EC), as the predecessor to the European Union was then called, deployed unarmed monitors to former Yugoslavia in the summer of 1991. UN peacekeepers entered Croatia in 1992 to protect Serb-populated areas and deployed to Bosnia in 1993 to protect mostly Muslim and Croat population centers. The UN- and EC-sponsored International Conference on the former Yugoslavia met repeatedly from 1992 onward. It spawned useful criteria for recognition of the former Yugoslav republics and resolved some succession issues, but it failed to produce the peace settlement sought.[3]

American attention to the Balkans in the 1990s is harder to explain. Few refugees made it across the Atlantic. Yugoslavia's six republics had a total population of under 24 million. Serbia, the largest of them, had close to 10 million, including 2 million in the autonomous province of Kosovo. Prewar Bosnia had 4.3 million, about twice the population of Macedonia. These were small places that did not threaten U.S. national security or offer significant economic opportunities. Yugoslavia's few natural resources were of little interest to Europe and even less to America. By the late 1980s, Socialist Yugoslavia was heavily indebted both internally and externally. Inflation and unemployment soared. Its economy was shrinking and its banks were folding.

Yugoslavia's Cold War strategic significance as a buffer between East and West had evaporated quickly after the fall of the Berlin Wall in 1989. There was no longer any geopolitical sense in Yugoslavia's policy of non-alignment, or strategic sense in vigorous American support for Socialist Yugoslavia. Secretary of State James Baker, on a trip to Belgrade to try to save Yugoslavia from dissolution, failed. His reaction was to declare that the United States had no dog in the fight to come.[4] The Balkans region was irrelevant to America's major interests, which lay in the reunification of Germany, the breakup of the Soviet Union, and the ongoing Israeli/Palestinian conflict, not to mention China and the Far East. American trade and investment with the region were minimal, its importance as a crossroads of Muslim and Christian civilization had faded, and its intricate politics and ethnic mosaic were mystifying.

The Balkans nevertheless returned to prominence. The fall of the Berlin Wall was a source of celebration in Europe and the United States, but scholars East and West predicted the emergence of ethnic and religious strife in the ruins of Communism.[5] Their worst fears did not materialize in the former Soviet Union, whose breakup was for the most part peaceful. But they did emerge in Socialist Yugoslavia, where opposition to Communism had taken ethnically "nationalist" forms. Most of the early leaders of what are now independent countries—Franjo Tuđman, Slobodan Milošević, Alija Izetbegović, and Ibrahim Rugova—were ethnic nationalists. They were concerned to assert Croat, Serb, Muslim, and Albanian identity, even if they differed in their intolerance toward other groups and their capacity to inflict harm.

Each felt his people aggrieved, mistreated, and discriminated against. Even Serbs, whom many other Yugoslavs regarded as demographically and politically dominant in Socialist Yugoslavia, felt ill-served. The Serbian Academy wrote in 1986:

> All nations are not equal: the Serbian nation, for example, did not obtain the right to its own state. Unlike national minorities, portions of the Serbian people, who live in other republics in large numbers, do not have the right to use their own language and alphabet, to organize politically and culturally, and to develop the unique culture of their nation.

> The unstoppable persecution of Serbs in Kosovo in a drastic manner shows that those principles that protect the autonomy of a minority (Albanians) are not applied when it comes to a minority within a minority (Serbs, Montenegrins, Turks and Gypsies in Kosovo).[6]

Socialist Yugoslavia was remarkably unsuccessful at convincing any of its ethnic groups that they were getting a fair shake.[7] All believed they were victims. Victimhood can be a prelude to violence, both for purposes of punishment and protection from real or imagined threats.[8] Thus was born the nationalist idea of providing protection to "all Serbs in one country" by incorporating into Serbia areas outside its borders where Serbs were in the majority or could be rendered the majority by chasing out the others who lived there.

The last, Western-oriented prime minister of Yugoslavia, Ante Marković, failed in his efforts to renegotiate the Yugoslav government's economic and financial relations with its six republics. The results were catastrophic. Slovenia's "ten-day" war for independence in 1991 gave way to Croatia's long, uphill struggle to regain control of its entire territory, parts of which were out of Zagreb's control and run by separatist Serbs under UN protection for more than three years. A Croatian *blitzkrieg* in 1995 and subsequent negotiations returned them to Croatian sovereignty. Bosnia slogged through three and a half years of war (1992–1995), with Muslims and Croats fighting each other part of the time, even while some of them fought together against Serbs. One hundred thousand of Bosnia's citizens died and half its population displaced. Kosovo lost fewer people—no more than 10,000—but saw more than a third of its population temporarily made refugees. Macedonia suffered a short Albanian rebellion in 2001. Montenegro escaped war on its own territory, but only with a lot of international assistance. Serbia, which lost wars in Slovenia, Croatia, Bosnia, and Kosovo, ended up absorbing hundreds of thousands of Serb refugees. Thus was the nationalist goal partly realized, with an ironic twist: they came to Serbia without the lands they had once called home in neighboring countries. This outcome rankles with more nationalist Serbs to this day.

American attention was partly due to the "CNN effect." Real-time news coverage from conflict zones was still a novelty, and it had a deep psychological impact. Photographs of emaciated inmates in Bosnian concentration camps could not be ignored, even if they were far less gruesome than what we see today on social media. Concentration camps were not supposed to happen in Europe: "Never again." That many of the victims were Muslim both attracted sympathy and generated concern about radicalization. American campuses organized to press the U.S. government for action on the Balkans. Bosnia had charismatic spokesmen in Haris Silajdžić, its wartime prime minister, and former Tulane University football player Muhamed Sacirbey (née Šaćirbegović), its UN ambassador. They were daily stars on American news broadcasts. Kosovo had the less charismatic but still photogenic Ibrahim Rugova, president of his internationally unrecognized and supposedly autonomous province. He had pledged to wear his silk scarf until independence.

At the U.S. State Department, Richard Holbrooke—made Assistant Secretary for Europe in September 1994—was determined to redeem the Cold War loss of Vietnam and demonstrate that American power could be projected to make good things happen in the post-Cold War world.[9] He and others worried that NATO risked irrelevance or worse if it failed to deal with a threat on Europe's doorstep, even if it was technically "out of area," the Cold War term for territory NATO was not obligated to defend.[10] Just before leaving office, President George H. W. Bush, who had intervened in late 1989 in Panama against a drug-trafficking president and in 1992 to relieve famine in Somalia, also threatened military intervention against Serbia if it caused conflict in Kosovo.[11] His successor, President Bill Clinton, promised during his first presidential campaign to intervene against Serbs in Bosnia, saying he would "lift" the arms embargo and "strike" the Bosnian Serb Army. He hesitated for more than three years, cautious in part because Secretary of State Warren Christopher failed to sell that idea to the Europeans. Unable to negotiate an end to the war, Europe did not want to "pour fuel on the fire next door."[12]

No single vital or strategic interest took the United States to war in the Balkans. Clinton's hesitation allowed an accumulation of secondary interests: preventing atrocities and refugee flows that might radicalize Balkan Muslims, calming domestic American reaction, maintaining U.S., EU, and NATO credibility, and reducing tensions within the Alliance. It was the combination of these that triggered American action.[13]

Bosnia eventually became a campaign issue. The Republican presidential candidate, Senator Robert Dole, started making political hay in the summer of 1995 by criticizing President Clinton for failing to follow through. Newly elected French President Jacques Chirac joined the chorus.[14] The die was cast. Acting to implement United Nations

Security Council Resolution 836 (1993) for protection of designated safe areas in Bosnia, the United States would use its vast military power in combination with its NATO allies to end the war and initiate two decades of U.S.- and EU-led postwar reconstruction, state-building, and peace-building.[15] Decades later, at the twentieth anniversary of the Dayton Accords, former President Clinton emphasized that Bosnia was the "canary in the coal mine" for a whole, free, peaceful, and democratic Europe.[16] Idealism had prevailed, albeit after a long delay.

The unipolar moment made it possible.[17] American power was uncontested in most of the world. The Bosnia success emboldened Washington. The United States intervened again in 1999 in Kosovo, where Milošević had instituted a reign of terror intended to chase Albanians from their homes and reclaim the "Serb Jerusalem." When a last-ditch negotiation at the Château de Rambouillet outside Paris failed, NATO again attacked from the air, supporting Kosovo Liberation Army insurgents on the ground. This time the Alliance acted without Security Council approval but with a wink and a nod from Boris Yeltsin's Russia, which in the endgame tried unsuccessfully to seize the Pristina airport but subsequently signed on to the Security Council resolution that ended the war.[18] Again the military effort succeeded, initiating another decade of postwar international state-building efforts, this time led by the UN.

There was ample historical precedent for war in the Balkans involving the Great Powers. The first (1912–1913) and second (1913) Balkan wars ushered in the twentieth century with a scramble for division of former Ottoman Empire territories. Soon thereafter, the assassination of Austrian Archduke Franz Ferdinand in Sarajevo triggered World War I. In World War II, the Balkans fell quickly to the Axis powers by June 1941. The Socialist Federal Republic of Yugoslavia emerged at the end of the war, after partisan leader Josip Broz "Tito" triumphed in a civil war over anti-Communist rivals. Throughout the Cold War, Socialist Yugoslavia remained a focus for the United States and NATO, because Tito defied the Soviet Union and achieved a measure of independence as a leader of the Non-Aligned Movement.

The facile explanation for the Balkan wars of the 1990s is "ancient hatreds," an idea that caused the Americans to hesitate to intervene.[19] You won't find that canard here. There have been episodes of inter-ethnic violence in the Balkans prior to the 1990s, but there have also been long periods of coexistence, co-operation, intermarriage, assimilation, and mutual assistance.[20] Balkan identities are remarkably fluid and multiple. You cannot tell the ethnic groups apart by looking at them (only a few ethnic nationalists make that claim). Their genetic heritage is indistinguishable, despite linguistic, cultural, religious, and other differences. The intolerance required to produce the wars of the 1990s is not indigenous, natural, or ancient.

Balkan ethnic nationalism is an example of Freud's "narcissism of small differences," magnified by political needs of the protagonists.[21] Conflict with neighbors on grounds of ethnic difference helped to keep Slobodan Milošević in power once the Soviet Union was gone. He encouraged Serbs to view the 1389 Battle of Kosovo Polje as the origin of their state and its antagonism with Albanians. But Albanians, who were not yet predominantly Muslims, fought on both sides of that battle with the advancing Ottomans, as did Serbs. It was only in the nineteenth century that a poet, Vuk Karadžić, provided the narrative that made the battle the foundation of Serbian nationalism.[22] There are ghosts needing exorcism in the Balkans, but they are not ancient ones.

Figure 2.1 attempts to structure the interlocking issues that brought war to the Balkans:

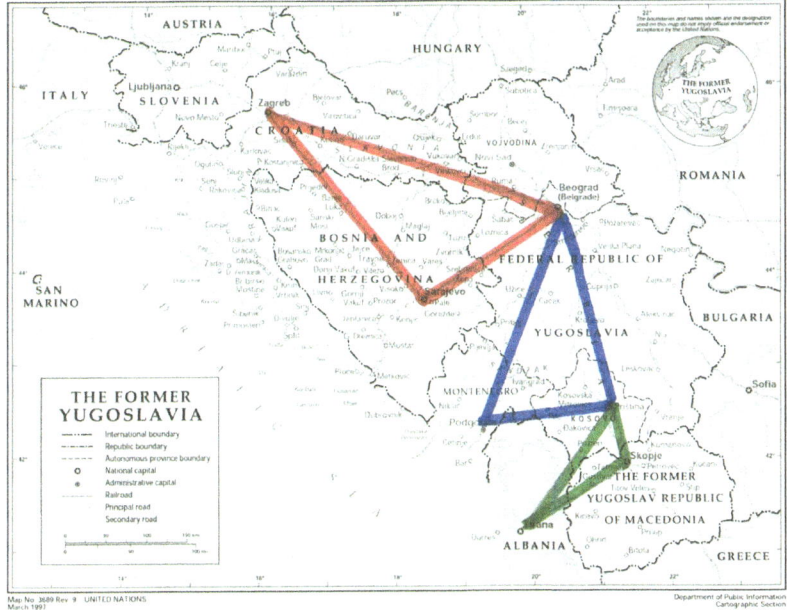

Fig. 2.1 The former Yugoslavia, dissected (United Nations)

The top triangle links the protagonists of the war in Bosnia: Belgrade, Sarajevo, and Zagreb. The main issue there was what the nineteenth century called "the Serbian question": Would Serbs live in several countries, or just one? That is where the United States tentatively entered the Balkans in 1994 to end fighting between Croats and Bosniaks (with a diplomatic agreement that created the Bosnian Federation) and more forcefully in 1995, when it intervened in the Bosnian War on behalf of those who wanted to preserve the country's sovereignty and territorial integrity.

The middle triangle links Belgrade, Pristina, and Podgorica (once Titograd, the capital of Montenegro), which were protagonists in the continuing dissolution of former Yugoslavia after Slovenia, Croatia, Macedonia, and Bosnia became independent in the early 1990s. That interlude ended with the independence of Montenegro in 2006 and of Kosovo in 2008.

The bottom triangle links Pristina, Skopje, and Tirana, the main players in what the nineteenth century regarded as "the Albanian question." That is the mirror image of the Serbian question that arose farther north: Will Albanians live in several countries, or in just one? While never asked as loudly as the Serbian question, the Albanian question remains open today, at least for some in the Balkans. It could still cause instability, if not war.

If the Balkans seem complicated and confusing, that is because they are. But there is nothing incomprehensible or even arcane about the driving factors, which exist elsewhere as well. War in the Balkans, as in many other parts of the world, is politics by other means. Distribution of power among ethnic nationalists was the main disagreement wherever we look in the region. Each group sought the means to protect itself from one or more of the others, whether the threats were real or imagined for political purposes.

Leadership and resources are important determinants of ethnic nationalism and its consequences. Montenegro's Milo Đukanović and Macedonia's Kiro Gligorov, while not immune to ethnic nationalism, tried to limit its impact on their small, weak, and poor countries. Both preferred to govern with the support of ethnic minorities. Some more ethnically nationalist leaders like Kosovo's Ibrahim Rugova and Bosnia's Alija Izetbegović still tried to keep their countries out of war and sought international intervention, not least because they lacked armies and were weaker than their antagonists. Croatia's Franjo Tuđman and Serbia's Slobodan Milošević were far stronger and bolder. Egged on by extremists, they sought confrontation because it consolidated their holds on power. They thought they had the means to win. They encouraged their ethnic compatriots to ask the classic Balkans question: Why should I live as a minority in your country when you can live as minority in mine?

Answering that question by building states that treat their citizens fairly and equally is one of the great challenges of our time. Failing to answer it means continuing to fight over where lines should be drawn between ethnic groups. That is a formula for long wars. There is always someone on the wrong side of the line. There is always a different line that would give one group more resources and another less. The problem arises not only in the Balkans but also in other parts of the former Ottoman Empire: Israel and Palestine, Iraq, Syria, Yemen, and Turkey. It also hovers over the conflict in Ukraine, where some Russian speakers who live in the southeast and Crimea prefer not to live in Ukraine as a minority but rather to live in Russia as part of the majority. The issues that arose in the Balkans were not unique to the Balkans. When not settled in advance, territorial partition, especially when attached to ethnicity or other identities, leads to conflict. The Balkans region is a good place to learn that and other lessons.

Some readers will doubt that the interventions in the Balkans have any claim on success. To them I recommend reading the quantitative analysis offered by RAND.[23] Of the twenty multilateral interventions since 1989, Bosnia and Kosovo were ranked the first and third most difficult, as measured by the calculated probability of returning to civil war within five years (respectively, 40 and 15%). They are still at peace. They have also shown marked improvement in democratization, governance, and prosperity, even if not as much as many might like. Macedonia, with only a 5% chance of returning to civil war within five years, is likewise at peace even if still troubled. It is also more prosperous and democratic than once it was, despite serious challenges. While it is arguable that conditions have deteriorated since RAND completed its work, the Balkans are still far better off than they were in the 1990s.

No one should deny that ethnic nationalism still plagues many Balkans countries. So too does the impulse of some of their leaders to restrict the press and abuse or even capture the state for personal gain.

Ethnic strife, constraints on the media, and corruption are real issues throughout the region. Slow economic growth, especially in the wake of the 2008 financial crisis, Greece's financial debacle, and the euro's shakiness, is also a major concern.

But we need to remember how the former Yugoslav republics began their existence as independent states: they were mostly poor, authoritarian, and ferociously conflictual. In the early 1990s it was dangerous to drive from one village to another in Bosnia. Today you can drive safely, except for a serious risk of traffic accidents, from Zagreb through Sarajevo to Podgorica, Pristina, and Skopje, then back through Belgrade. That is remarkable. The roads are little improved, but the environment is. The trip wasn't possible from about 1991 through at the least 2001. The cities mentioned are now the capitals of middle-income, illiberal democracies where large-scale conflict is rare or nonexistent. Slovenia and Croatia are members in pretty good standing of NATO and the EU. Montenegro and Serbia are candidates for EU accession. Albania and Macedonia are expected to start negotiations in 2019. Even some laggards know where they want to end up. Macedonia and Kosovo have NATO aspirations and share the goal of eventually entering the EU.

The Balkan countries are much smaller in population (and land area) than Iraq and Afghanistan, where American-led efforts in the wake of invasion and occupation have been far less successful. Relative to their size, we deployed more troops (about 100 times more per capita) and spent far more (on the order of ten times more per capita) in the Balkans, even if the total expended by the United States (about $25–30 billion) represents only a few months of war in Afghanistan and Iraq at their peak. The Balkan peace- and state-building efforts were unintentional experiments in what could be achieved if adequate resources were devoted to the task. The United States and Europe not only intervened but also acted jointly to guarantee peace agreements that otherwise might have quickly frayed. The fact that we are no longer willing or able to match that level of resources and commitment rightly gives pause about undertaking future efforts.

There is little danger of that for now. President Barack Obama was determined to avoid the slippery slope into what he termed nation-building, most notably in Syria, a country of close to 22 million before the war that has spewed more than the 5.6 million officially registered refugees into its neighbors, in addition to displacing half the Syrians who remain in the country. President Donald Trump has reiterated the refusal to do nation-building and says he wants to withdraw from Syria altogether. The Europeans are hesitating even to disembark in Libya, a country today of not more than 6 million people, closer to Balkan dimensions and amply endowed with oil and gas that could ease the process and reward European efforts. No one wants to take on reconstruction in Yemen, a poverty-stricken country of 26 million embroiled in multiple wars.

What are the alternatives to reconstruction and state-building, which are now so out of fashion? Returning to habit, Europeans and Americans are for the moment inclined to hope that an authoritarian like Egypt's President Abdel Fattah el-Sisi can restore order rather than risk a democratic transition. The West may also simply stand by and monitor state collapse, as in Libya, or provide humanitarian assistance to ease the plight of civilians and assuage our own consciences, as in Syria. Or we may allow or support neighboring countries to intervene, as Saudi Arabia and the United Arab Emirates are doing in Yemen. All three approaches were tried in the Balkans, without success. Only Great Power–led, multilateral intervention with the United States and the EU acting in tandem worked. It remains to be seen whether the alternatives will be more successful in the Middle East.

There is already no lack of intervention in the Middle East as well as in Ukraine. But the military interventions in Libya (led by Egypt and the United Arab Emirates), Yemen (led by Saudi Arabia), Syria (by Russia and Iran as well as Turkey and the United States), and Ukraine (by Russia) are not the sort that led to relatively stable outcomes in the Balkans. Nor are they likely to be successful. Carefully documented experience suggests that what works is impartial intervention with civilian as well as military means, agreed multilateral Great Power engagement, and consent of the warring parties.[24] That is what benefited the Balkans. Russian unilateral intervention in Ukraine, which is far from impartial and without the consent of the Ukrainian government, has little chance of success, if that is defined as ending the war and allowing peace- and state-building to proceed. The multiple interventions in Syria, Egypt's in Libya, and the Saudi/Emirati intervention in Yemen are also unlikely to lead to stable and peaceful outcomes. Insurgencies of the sort that now plague these countries often last for ten years or more.[25] Without a dramatic change in attitudes, today's interventions are unlikely to come close to the benefits of those conducted in the 1990s in the Balkans.

While out of fashion, multilateral intervention supported—or at least not opposed—by the Great Powers and undertaken from an impartial stance with the consent of main protagonists will someday somewhere again be judged desirable and feasible. Interim government or even international administration, as in Bosnia and Kosovo, is likely to be required.[26] Success and failure in these situations is highly context dependent. Russian and Turkish troops have already policed "de-escalation" zones inside Syria. The United States has sponsored training for police and establishment of a governing body for Raqqa in Syria's east, which American-allied forces dominate. Many Western analysts have argued for an international peacekeeping deployment to Libya, where a UN-sponsored Government of National Accord has failed to exert its authority, or even protect itself from attack, without international intervention. An eventual political settlement in Yemen will likewise need substantial international support, both civilian and military, and even possible international administration. The Europeans and Russia are discussing the possibility of deploying UN peacekeepers in Ukraine, where international observers deployed by the Organization for Security and Co-operation in Europe are already active.

So even if Washington, Brussels, and Moscow would like in principle to avoid state-building in today's conflict zones, they are already on the slippery slope to doing it, albeit often without the resources and consensus needed for success. Understanding the Balkans experience, a relatively successful one even if not yet completed, can help to calibrate and target what can be done in the Middle East, Ukraine, and elsewhere.

Notes

1. Paul B. Stares, "Preventive Priorities Survey, 2018," Council on Foreign Relations, New York (December 2017), https://www.cfr.org/sites/default/files/report_pdf/PPS_2018_Web.pdf.
2. Ivo H. Daalder, *Getting to Dayton: The Making of America's Bosnia Policy* (Washington, DC: Brookings Institution, 2000).
3. Bertrand G. Ramcharan, *The International Conference on the Former Yugoslavia: Official Papers* (The Hague: Den Haag, 1997).
4. Robert L. Hutchings, *American Diplomacy and the End of the Cold War: An Insider's Account of US Diplomacy in Europe, 1989–1992* (Washington, DC: Woodrow Wilson Center Press, 1997). President George H. W. Bush felt the same way. See Hal Brands, *Making the*

Unipolar Moment: U.S. Foreign Policy and the Rise of the Post-Cold War Order (Ithaca: Cornell University Press, 2016), 323.
5. Stephen Van Evera, "Hypotheses on Nationalism and War," *International Security* 18, no. 4 (1994). https://doi.org/10.2307/2539176.
6. There is an English translation of the draft (it was never finalized): "Serbian Academy of Arts and Sciences (SANU) Memorandum, 1986," http://chnm.gmu.edu/1989/items/show/674. For the role of Serbian nationalism, see Sonja Biserko, *Yugoslavia's Implosion: The Fatal Attraction of Serbian Nationalism* (Oslo: Norwegian Helsinki Committee, 2012), http://www.helsinki.org.rs/doc/yugoslavias%20implosion.pdf.
7. Susan L. Woodward, *Balkan Tragedy: Chaos and Dissolution After the Cold War* (Washington, DC: Brookings Institution, 1997).
8. Daniel Bar-Tal, Lily Chernyak-Hai, Noa Schori, and Ayelet Gunda, "A Sense of Self-Perceived Collective Victimhood in Intractable Conflicts," *International Review of the Red Cross* 91, no. 874 (June 2009), https://www.icrc.org/eng/assets/files/other/irrc-874-bartal-chernyakhai-schori-gundar.pdf. For the Balkans specifically, see David Bruce MacDonald, *Balkan Holocausts? Serbian and Croatian Victim Centred Propaganda and the War in Yugoslavia* (Manchester: Manchester University Press, 2002).
9. Marvin Kalb and Deborah Kalb, "Clinton: The First Baby-Boomer President," in *Haunting Legacy: Vietnam and the American Presidency from Ford to Obama* (Washington, DC: Brookings Institution, 2011), 150–85.
10. Richard G. Lugar, "NATO: Out of Area or Out of Business: A Call for US Leadership to Revive and Redefine the Alliance" (Remarks delivered to the Open Forum of the US Department of State, August 2, 1993).
11. Michael S. Lund, "Preventive Diplomacy for Macedonia, 1992–1999: From Containment to Nation Building," in *Opportunities Missed, Opportunities Seized: Preventive Diplomacy in the Post-Cold War World*, ed. Bruce W. Jentleson (Lanham, MD: Rowman & Littlefield, 2000), 173–208.
12. That is the phrase Prime Minister Azeglio Ciampi used in rejecting Christopher's proposal when I accompanied the secretary to call on the prime minister in 1993.
13. Daniel Serwer, "U.S. Policy on the Western Balkans," in *Unfinished Business: The Western Balkans and the International Community*, ed. Vedran Dzihic and Daniel Hamilton (Washington, DC: Center for Transatlantic Relations, 2012), 221–29.
14. William Safire, "Essay; Clinton Abdicates as Leader," *New York Times*, July 27, 1995. https://www.nytimes.com/1995/07/27/opinion/essay-clinton-abdicates-as-leader.html.

15. "NATO/IFOR: UN Resolution S/RES/836 (1993)," https://www.nato.int/ifor/un/u930604a.htm.
16. "20th Anniversary of Dayton Peace Accords: Bill Clinton Keynote Address," YouTube, Flyer News, November 30, 2015, https://www.youtube.com/watch?v=ZGI1C9GdKf0.
17. Charles Krauthammer, "The Unipolar Moment," *Foreign Affairs* 70, no. 1 (1991), https://www.foreignaffairs.com/articles/1991-02-01/unipolar-moment. For the evolution of the unipolar moment, see Hal Brands, *Making the Unipolar Moment: U.S. Foreign Policy and the Rise of the Post-Cold War Order* (Ithaca: Cornell University Press, 2016).
18. Strobe Talbott, interview, "War in Europe," Frontline, Public Broadcasting Service (2016), http://www.pbs.org/wgbh/pages/frontline/shows/kosovo/interviews/talbott.html.
19. Robert D. Kaplan, *Balkan Ghosts: A Journey through History* (New York: St. Martin's Press, 1996). Kaplan himself has disowned the anti-interventionist policy slant his book is said to have caused; see his 1996 foreword, x–xii.
20. For wartime examples, read Tito's granddaughter's account: Svetlana Broz, *Good People in an Evil Time: Portraits of Complicity and Resistance in the Bosnian War*, ed. Laurie Kain Hart, trans. Ellen Elias-Bursać (New York: Other Press, 2005).
21. Sigmund Freud, *Civilization and Its Discontents* (New York: Norton, 1962), 58–63. Michael Ignatieff applies Freud's "narcissism of small differences" to the Bosnian War in *The Warrior's Honor: Ethnic War and the Modern Conscience* (New York: Metropolitan Books, 1998).
22. Michael Anthony Sells, *The Bridge Betrayed: Religion and Genocide in Bosnia* (Berkeley: University of California Press, 1996), 37–39.
23. James Dobbins, Laurel E. Miller, Stephanie Pezard, Christopher S. Chivvis, Julie E. Taylor, Keith Crane, Calin Trenkov-Wermuth, and Tewodaj Mengistu, *Overcoming Obstacles to Peace: Local Factors in Nation-Building* (Santa Monica, CA: RAND, 2013). https://www.rand.org/pubs/research_reports/RR167.html. Also available in print form.
24. Patrick Regan, *Civil Wars and Foreign Powers: Outside Intervention in Intrastate Conflict* (Ann Arbor: University of Michigan Press, 2000).
25. Ben Connable and Martin C. Libicki, *How Insurgencies End* (Santa Monica, CA: RAND, 2010), https://www.rand.org/pubs/monographs/MG965.html. Also available in print form.
26. Karen Guttieri and Jessica Piombo, *Interim Governments: Institutional Bridges to Peace and Democracy?* (Washington, DC: United States Institute of Peace Press, 2007); See also Richard Caplan, *International Governance of War-Torn Territories* (New York: Oxford University Press, 2005).

Open Access This chapter is distributed under the terms of the Creative Commons Attribution 4.0 International License (http://creativecommons.org/licenses/by/4.0/), which permits use, duplication, adaptation, distribution and reproduction in any medium or format, as long as you give appropriate credit to the original author(s) and the source, a link is provided to the Creative Commons license and any changes made are indicated.

The images or other third party material in this chapter are included in the work's Creative Commons license, unless indicated otherwise in the credit line; if such material is not included in the work's Creative Commons license and the respective action is not permitted by statutory regulation, users will need to obtain permission from the license holder to duplicate, adapt or reproduce the material.

CHAPTER 3

Bosnia: Prelude, Disease, and Sequelae

Abstract In Bosnia, three factors led to war: the breakup of former Yugoslavia, Slobodan Milošević's political ambitions and military capability, and ethnic nationalism, particularly in its territorial form. It is hard to picture the Bosnian War without any one of these. It is hard to picture peace prevailing with all three. After an initial period of stalemate, the postwar process in Bosnia benefited for almost ten years from ample international commitment of political will and other resources, blocking of Croatia's support for Croat separatism inside Bosnia, and co-optation of Bosnian elites. The state- and peace-building process stalled thereafter, as the Americans passed the baton to a Europe that fumbled it. Bosnia is still not yet safe from nationalist and Russian destabilization.

Keywords Dayton peace agreements · Ethnic cleansing · High Representative

Former Yugoslavia was a weak state.[1] It lacked legitimacy with its people, its inefficient socialist economic system was creaking, and leaders of its multiple ethnic groups were developing separate "national" cultural and historical narratives that competed with Yugoslav identity, which had a tenuous hold once Tito died in 1980. The fall of the Berlin Wall undermined the centralized authority of the Communist Party that still held Yugoslavia together, albeit tenuously. The dominant "Socialist" ideology was cosmopolitan and multiethnic but still autocratic. Internal opposition to it was largely organized along ethnic lines, starting in the late 1960s. Each of what Yugoslavs called the "national" (ethnic) narratives included a large slice of persecution by the others: Serbs by Albanians in Kosovo; Croats, Slovenes, and Bosniak Muslims by Serbian political, linguistic, and cultural hegemony throughout Yugoslavia; and Albanians by being excluded and marginalized politically and culturally in Kosovo, Serbia, and Macedonia.

Milošević had made a career entirely as an apparatchik within the Yugoslav communist hierarchy.[2] He was late to the nationalist discourse, but he adopted it, initially to recentralize the Yugoslav state, and later to acquire power in Serbia and preserve as much of Yugoslavia as possible under Serbian rule. Late though he was, Milošević was ruthless in using Serbian nationalism to reestablish tight control over Vojvodina and Kosovo, the two autonomous provinces inside Serbia, as well as over Montenegro, one of the six republics that made up Yugoslavia when it was reestablished in the wake of World War II. Had Serbian nationalism remained an intellectual movement of the sort espoused in the Serbian Academy's draft memorandum, it is doubtful it could have played any significant role in breaking up Yugoslavia. But Milošević was able to translate this academic language into a rallying cry that mobilized Serbs against the autonomous provinces, against the federal government, against the other republics, and in favor of a country dominated by Serbs. He had the territorial ambition and military capability to back up the rhetoric.

Slovenia, where few Serbs lived, was the most prosperous of Socialist Yugoslavia's six republics and the keystone of their federation. Once the Berlin Wall fell, Slovenes were no longer prepared to see their finances drained to benefit Yugoslavs who lived in Macedonia and Kosovo. They voted for independence in a December 1990 referendum. The Yugoslav National Army (JNA) lost the ten-day war that ensued. Milošević withdrew it to concentrate on republics where Serbs were a larger proportion of the population.

Inter-ethnic violence in Croatia was already on the rise. Led by Franjo Tuđman, a JNA general turned Croat nationalist historian, Zagreb followed Ljubljana in organizing and approving secession from Yugoslavia in May 1991. Many Serbs, including in the United States, believe that Washington conspired with Ljubljana and Zagreb to dismantle former Yugoslavia. But that was not the case. In Belgrade in June 1991

Secretary Baker even said publicly that Washington would not recognize Slovenian or Croatian independence "under any circumstances."[3] He was still trying to avoid what soon became inevitable. By early 1992, the Maastricht Treaty had created the European Union (previously known as the European Community) and its Common Foreign and Security Policy. Germany insisted that other EU members recognize Slovenia and Croatia or risk scuttling the newly created Union. Even Rome and London, which almost always found ways of following the American lead on important issues, instead defied Washington and complied with Germany's diktat. So too did the rest of the EU.

Bosnia and Macedonia might both have preferred to stay in Yugoslavia, but with the exit of Slovenia and Croatia it was clear that Milošević and Serbian nationalism would dominate whatever was left of the Yugoslav Federation. Bosnian President Alija Izetbegović had not advocated an independent Bosnia or, as charged in the 1980s in a Yugoslav court, an ethnically cleansed Muslim territory, or as charged later, an Islamic Republic.[4] His *Islamic Declaration* was about Muslim moral regeneration and education in the modern world, not politics. He was acutely aware that Bosnia lacked an army and would face daunting odds if it tried to secede.[5]

But Izetbegović was not in control of events. Slovenia and Croatia were already independent. With little provocation, Serb-majority parts of Bosnia had called for help and protection from Belgrade, which provided ample support through the JNA. In January 1992 the nationalist Serbs conducted their own referendum to secede from a Bosnia that was not yet independent. This pattern—a minority population that constitutes a majority on particular territory calling on its "mother" country for protection and conducting a referendum on secession—is a classic irredentist technique that would be repeated decades later in Crimea.

Aiming to promote liberal democracy based on individual rights throughout the Balkans, the Badinter Commission, a creature of the International Conference on Yugoslavia, had established a majority referendum in each Yugoslav republic as one of several prerequisites for independence.[6] Brussels accordingly insisted on a majority-rules referendum in all of Bosnia, held on February 29 and March 1, 1992. Virtually 100% voted for independence, but only 63.4% of registered voters went to the polls, most of whom were Bosniaks and Croats. Many Serbs boycotted, believing that would invalidate the result, an expectation based on the group-rights practice of Socialist Yugoslavia. Ethnic cleansing of Muslims and Croats from Serb-dominated areas that claimed to have seceded (based on a referendum in which Muslims and Croats had not participated) had already begun. Izetbegović, who lacked an army, nevertheless went ahead and declared independence almost immediately, likely hoping that would bring international help. War was on.

It was a brutal, lengthy, and deadly disaster. The highlights tell only a small fraction of the story: one hundred thousand people killed, half the population displaced from their homes, town centers reduced to rubble by small-arms fire, Sarajevo nearly split in two and almost defeated in the first weeks, then under siege and bombarded for three long years, Izetbegović kidnapped and exchanged for a JNA military contingent attacked by a still rudimentary Bosnian Army while under UN protection, the murder of more than seven thousand Muslim males captured in the UN-protected "safe area" of Srebrenica.[7] Croats and Bosniaks began the war united in favor of an independent Bosnia, but from June 1992 until February 1994 they fought against each other in central and southern Bosnia even while fighting together against the Serbs along the Posavina corridor in the north. Tuđman and Milošević might have liked to divide Bosnia between them, but they had no idea what to do with the Bosniak population except chase it from territory Croats and Serbs controlled, which threatened to create the conditions for an Islamic statelet (or two) in central Bosnia.

Europe and the UN had tried to find a solution to the conflict even before it broke out. In this case, prevention as well as their efforts after the outbreak of war failed, because the means available were not sufficient to meet the challenge.[8] In 1991, while trying to negotiate an end to the Slovenian war for independence, EU President Jacque Poos declared that "the hour of Europe has dawned." It turned out to be a long and dark hour in Bosnia, as the Europeans were not prepared to intervene militarily and the Americans were focused elsewhere.[9] Initiatives like the Owen/Stoltenberg and Vance/Owen plans, which in many respects foreshadowed the eventual power-sharing settlement reached at Dayton, not only failed to bring about an end to the war but likely caused ethnic cleansing by identifying parts of the country that would be designated "Croat," "Serb," and "Bosniak."[10] Courageous Europeans staffing the EU's own monitoring mission as well as a large part of the UN peacekeeping force could do nothing to alter the long stalemate that persisted from 1992 until NATO intervened in 1995.

They reported on what was going on and protected humanitarian convoys, but little more.

The UN and the Americans did a bit better. In early 1994 they cooperated in convincing Tuđman that chasing the Bosniaks from Croat-dominated areas would create something he would not like on his borders. In the State Department it was called "a non-viable, rump Islamic Republic that would be a platform for Iranian-sponsored terrorism in Europe." Islamic terrorism in the United States had not yet been invented, even in our imaginations. Nor was extremism common among Bosnian Muslims. Tuđman was fond of claiming that civilization stopped at the Sava, the river that forms the northern border of Bosnia and Croatia. The Americans wondered on which side of the Sava it stopped. Asked if they are Sunni or Shia, Bosniaks often reply with puzzlement, No, we are Bosnian. But after three years of war in which people were killed because they were Muslim, there was a small but growing group of radicals, in addition to hundreds of people the Americans called "muj" (mujahideen) who had come from abroad to assist. Initially multiethnic, the Bosnian Army had become an almost entirely Bosniak army.[11] After the war, NATO raided at least one terrorist training facility.

To avoid a rump Islamic state, Washington proposed Tuđman cooperate with the Muslims in fighting the secessionist Serbs. The deal was sweetened with the one-quarter to one-third of the arms the Croatians skimmed from shipments to the Bosnian Army from Turkey, Iran, Malaysia, and other countries, in contravention of a UN arms embargo. The Americans turned a blind eye to the arms smuggling, hoping to strengthen both Croat and Bosniak forces for the fight against the Serbs.[12] In public the Americans said they were trying to preserve multiethnic democracy in Bosnia, but this idealistic formulation was combined, at least for the realists, with prevention of terrorism.

That perspective still has validity today: any partition of Bosnia would necessarily be at least three-way, leaving one if not two rump Islamic states at its center (surrounding Bihać and Sarajevo). Multiethnicity is now the less compelling argument, as the wars in Bosnia homogenized much of its population. But potential radicalization is a far stronger argument than it was twenty years ago, as Islamist extremism has grown as a threat to both the United States and Europe. Bosnia's contribution to foreign fighters in Syria and Iraq includes both extremists who fought in the 1990s and more recent recruits.[13]

The political outcome of Tuđman's recognition of the risk of creating an Islamic state was the Bosnian Federation: a constitutional arrangement between the Croats and Bosniaks intended to govern on at least 51% of the territory, eventually to be confederated to Croatia (a promise never fulfilled).[14] The other 49% was to be the "other entity": Republika Srpska (Serb Republic, to be distinguished however from the Republic of Serbia, Bosnia's neighbor to the east with its capital in Belgrade). The Serbs might also have benefited from an arrangement with the Bosniaks like the one the Croats had, but Milošević was never convinced of what today is obvious to all the Serbian foreign ministry officials: partition of Bosnia resulting in an Islamic republic is a terrible idea.[15]

The Federation was a military success. Amity between Croats and Bosniaks was not the basis for its advances in the summer of 1995. The mostly Muslim Bosnian Army and the mostly Catholic Croat Defence Council (HVO) both fought against the Serbs but competed for territory. They assumed they would be able to keep whatever they conquered. Neither would have succeeded alone or without NATO air attacks and the Croatian Army, which not only supplied the HVO but also commanded it.

NATO's contribution was the bombing of the Bosnian Serb Army (VRS), precipitated in August 1995 by shelling of Sarajevo. That triggered what were known as the "Goražde rules," which required a NATO response if any of the six UN-protected areas in Bosnia were attacked.[16] This agreed trip wire precipitated action. But NATO quickly ran out of primary and secondary targets when the Serbs parked their armor and artillery next to mosques and schools. When it turned to lower-priority targets it started hitting the communication nodes of the VRS, which were vital to the ability of its relatively small force to counter the much larger Bosnian Army along a lengthy confrontation line. The VRS retreated rapidly.[17] The Federation forces, which had controlled less than 30% of the territory during more than three years of war, soon overran more than two-thirds.

This is where "Dayton" comes in. The word has come to signify the end of the seemingly intractable violence in Bosnia from 1992 to 1995. The narrative surrounding it is powerful: after everyone else (the UN, the Europeans) had tried and failed, the United States intervened with military force and an American diplomat took the warring parties off to an isolated air force base in Ohio, where he bent them to his will and ended the war.[18] Holbrooke left no doubt that the critical moment was when Yugoslav President Slobodan Milošević agreed to accept peace with the Federation (Bosniak and Croat) forces arrayed against him and the army of Republika Srpska.[19] This was the triumph of American statecraft, force, and will, wielded together in a good cause against a destructive force.

The "Dayton" narrative is powerful but inaccurate and misleading.[20] It has led diplomats down the wrong paths ever since, causing them to overestimate the decisiveness of the use of force, which was necessary but not sufficient. Holbrooke's team interpreted what had happened as Milošević's reaction to the NATO bombing of the Serb forces in Bosnia. But Milošević did not care much about the Serb forces in Bosnia, which were mainly loyal not to him but to the Bosnian Serb leader Radovan Karadžić, who at the time was regarded as a potential rival to Milošević in Belgrade, if Republika Srpska were to become part of Serbia.[21] Belgrade had run out of the money needed to finance the war in Bosnia. Milošević wanted sanctions lifted.[22]

The reality of Dayton was thus different from Holbrooke's narrative. Milošević came to Dayton suing for peace.[23] He was responding not to the bombing per se but rather to a threat to his own hold on power. He had believed that the Serbs in Croatia could hold their own against the Croatian Army.[24] They failed. As a result, something like two hundred thousand Serbs had walked out of Croatia into Serbia only a few months earlier, when Zagreb launched its Operation Storm to regain control of UN-Protected Areas in Croatia. By late September 1995, the Federation forces were routing the VRS. Milošević told the Americans he was concerned about another flood of refugees. Anyone who took that as an expression of humanitarian consciousness had misunderstood. What really concerned Milošević was the prospect of another five hundred thousand (or more) Serbs walking out of Bosnia into Serbia, where they would have joined the Croatian Serbs in calling for his ouster.[25]

When Milošević came to Dayton he needed an agreement and the sanctions relief he had been trying to negotiate with the Americans for months, unsuccessfully.[26] Imposition of the sanctions years earlier had not much affected him. This is typical: sanctions rarely have an immediate effect, but their removal can be a powerful incentive.[27] For Milošević, sanctions relief became urgent as the tide of war turned against his forces. But the man was cagey and feigned resistance until the last moment, a standard Balkans practice, getting in the process a good deal for Republika Srpska that undermined his rival Karadžić, whom the Americans and Milošević had arranged to exclude from Dayton.

Milošević's gains included 49% of the territory of Bosnia and Herzegovina, forcing the Federation forces to roll back from the more than two-thirds that they controlled when the cease-fire finally went into effect. He also got international acceptance of Republika Srpska, an "entity" defined by its majority Serb population, even though its territory was not majority Serb before the war. Autonomous and entitled to special relations with Serbia, Republika Srpska kept its army, police, and other security forces, which were saved from almost certain defeat. The central government (in Bosnia called the "state" government) had few functions, the execution of which was constrained by ethnically based vetoes. These power-sharing arrangements were codified in a difficult-to-amend, permanent constitution that the Americans insisted upon, fearing that anything easier to revise would lead to partition. All armies and ethnic nationalists on the verge of defeat should have the good fortune to be hauled off to "Dayton."

The Croats also got a very good deal at Dayton. Tuđman was in the driver's seat, as the successful Federation offensive was due in part to his forces backing up as well as commanding the Bosnian Croats. He controlled the only routes into the Bosniak areas of central Bosnia and skimmed off arms there. The Croats got what they asked for: half the Federation and one-third of the state government in Sarajevo, even though they had been only 17% of the population before the war and were certainly far less than that at the time of Dayton. They are now officially 15.4% of a significantly reduced total population, while Bosniaks are 51.1%.[28]

The Croats also asked that the Americans get the Bosniaks to expel the foreign mujahideen imported to fight in some units of the Bosnian Army. When asked how many there were, Jadranko Prlić—then the "defense minister" associated with the Croat parastate known as "Herzeg-Bosna," created to govern on HVO-controlled territory during the war—said seven hundred.[29] This should be regarded as an upper limit of the number, which in subsequent years has been grossly inflated into the thousands by those who want to portray Bosnia as a haven for Muslim extremists. For months after Dayton, the CIA produced regular reports on whether the Bosniaks were complying. Half of the "muj" were forced to leave Bosnia. Some were difficult to expel because they had married Bosnians and had Bosnian children. When asked whether the CIA would produce comparable reports on expulsion of non-Bosnian Serbs (mainly from Serbia) who led and staffed units of the VRS, the answer was no. Getting rid of foreign fighters meant Muslims, not Serbs or Croats.

It wasn't Milošević's or Tuđman's arm that Holbrooke needed to twist at Dayton. It was Izetbegović's. The Bosniak president said it clearly at the initialing of the Dayton agreements, as he had previously to Holbrooke in private: "It is not a just peace ... but my people need peace."[30] In addition to the weakened power-sharing government in Sarajevo, Izetbegović was forced to accept Republika Srpska on nearly half the country's territory in exchange for a promise that all refugees and displaced people would be able to return to their homes. He certainly knew how difficult that promise would be to fulfill in an entity that defined itself as "Serb" and had removed most of its non-Serb population during the war. Republika Srpska, which in 2013 was more than 80% Serb, would not be majority Serb if everyone were to return to their prewar homes. Dayton confirmed Serb military successes that were in danger on the battlefield. Izetbegović was a man of few and bitter words, but not a fool.

Snatching defeat, or at least a mixed result, from the jaws of victory is the phrase that comes to mind. Why did the Americans do it? Anxious to end the war, they believed that a temporary compromise with territorial ethnic nationalism could be converted eventually to a more liberal democratic order.[31] Why did Izetbegović allow it? America was his ally and chief, though not only, diplomatic backer in the war. They made it clear they would not continue to support him if he refused the settlement. Izetbegović assumed that Washington could turn off the Saudi money that flowed into his bank account. The story Holbrooke's team told him—that U.S. intelligence sources had concluded that Serb resistance was stiffening and would throw back the Federation offensive—would have sounded plausible to Izetbegović, as the Bosnian Army overextended itself several times during the war and suffered ignominious defeats as a result. But this time the story was made up out of whole cloth.[32] In addition, the Americans offered Izetbegović something he found hard to turn down: a massive "equip and train" program for the Federation armed forces that would at least guarantee that something like the stalemated 1992–1995 war would not happen again. Once the Americans had convinced Milošević and Tuđman to sign on, Izetbegović could not be the odd one out.

Dayton, rather than being a triumph of American diplomacy in a good cause, is more like an object lesson in why you should not be America's best friend. If you are, the Americans find it easier to twist your arm than that of your enemy. There was no bright new idea in the Dayton agreements. They largely confirmed governing arrangements that already existed at the entity level and superimposed a weak central government based on power sharing among former warring parties. Holbrooke's key contribution was not conceptual but rather his ability to point all the levers of American power in the same direction at the same time. Secretaries of state and even presidents have difficulty doing that, never mind an assistant secretary of state. The situation was not naturally "ripe" for resolution. Neither a mutually hurting stalemate nor a mutually enticing opportunity, which scholars view as preconditions for a negotiated agreement, existed in Bosnia before the Dayton talks. Holbrooke ripened the situation by making it impossible for Izetbegović to continue fighting, while providing Milošević and Tuđman with good reasons to stop.

The main issues resolved at Dayton were territorial and constitutional: the agreements separated the Federation and Republika Srpska by an "inter-entity boundary line." Dayton also imposed power-sharing arrangements and mutual vetoes, without, however, any provision for improving inter-ethnic relations. The agreements included provisions for transitional justice, to be conducted mainly by the International Criminal Tribunal for the former Yugoslavia in The Hague, but little else to give an accounting for what had happened and why. Dayton validated the existence of Republika Srpska, abolished the Yugoslav-origin Bosnian Republic that Izetbegović had led during the war, and enabled the ethnic nationalists responsible for the war to remain in power. Negotiated agreements necessarily involve painful compromises. Many of Bosnia's postwar problems stem directly from the power-sharing arrangements that diplomats and scholars think so necessary to negotiating an end to civil wars.[33]

Now it is more than two decades years later. Even if the peace was not just, or warm, it was the absence of war and it has held. What can we learn from the postwar experience? First and foremost is that implementation is as important as the peace agreement. There had been no peace process to speak of leading up to Dayton. What we normally think of as the peace process—the warring parties getting to know each other, learning their adversary's language and tricks, finding out what is feasible and what is not, learning what they can trust and not—happened in Bosnia mostly after the signing, not before. The Americans—who believed that civilian interference in military operations was a major cause of UN failure in Bosnia from 1992 to 1995—insisted at Dayton that the NATO military commander in Bosnia report exclusively through the normal NATO command to the (American) Supreme Allied Commander. This was intended to prevent "mission creep" and civilian interference as well as fend off the French, who were then not participating in the NATO military chain of command and wanted it modified to suit their preferences in Bosnia. This sharp division between the international civilian and military efforts severely hampered what became known as "Dayton implementation."

The Europeans were put in charge of the civilian side, intentionally kept as separate as possible, through an international community High Representative, initially Carl Bildt, former prime minister and future foreign minister of Sweden. While they later came to appreciate Bildt, at Dayton the Americans were anxious to exclude him from anything that might prove important, especially military implementation of the agreement. Not surprisingly, many of the most severe problems in the first years after the war arose precisely in the interface between military and civilian responsibilities, which the Americans were so desperate to separate. Capture of war criminals, return of displaced people and refugees, and freedom of movement required tight coordination between military and civilians, not strict separation. The turnover of the so-called "Serb suburbs" of Sarajevo to the Federation was an early indicator of how difficult things would be. None of these areas had more than a plurality of Serbs before the war, and one area was adjacent to downtown. The Republika Srpska authorities asked for and got permission from NATO to keep their police in these areas, claiming that this would encourage Serbs to stay. They then used the police to "self-cleanse" Serbs, moving them out of Sarajevo in NATO-supplied vehicles while burning and flooding high-rise apartments so that they would be uninhabitable.[34]

Implementation of the Dayton agreements in the first couple of years proved too hard.[35] Republika Srpska tried to prevent the Sarajevo state government that the Dayton accords created from any sort of authority in the 49% of the territory it controlled. The Bosnian Croats tried to preserve their separate wartime "Herzeg-Bosna" institutions. The Bosniaks tried to push return of displaced Muslims into strategically sensitive areas in Republika Srpska and Herzeg-Bosna, even while they resisted returns of Croats and Serbs to Sarajevo. As a result, in December 1997 the Peace Implementation Council, the committee of governments that still oversees the peace process, granted to the High Representative "Bonn powers" to issue legislation and to remove officials from office. The powerless High Representative became a virtual autocrat charged with preserving the peace and getting Bosnia to democracy.

Then began an intensive period of civilian peace implementation under European leadership with strong American backing, beginning with Wolfgang Petritsch (1999–2002) and culminating with Paddy Ashdown (2002–2006) as High Representative. Some of Bosnia's war criminals were removed from office, the Sarajevo state government was strengthened, decently organized elections were held repeatedly, the armed forces were shrunk and mostly unified, the police were reformed and vetted more than once, the central bank and currency were established, some displaced people and refugees returned home, and property rights were clarified. Ashdown dismantled Herzeg-Bosna, thus blocking the worst of Croatia's meddling.[36] Nothing comparable was done with Serbia, which continued to wield undue influence in Republika Srpska. The economy grew rapidly for several years after Dayton from its low wartime base, and by the time of the international financial crisis in 2008 it had reached about three times its GNP at the end of the war, making Bosnia an "upper middle income" country.[37] With a lot of heavy lifting by the Americans, Bosnia even had an avowedly anti-nationalist prime minister for a year or so. The Europeans provided most of the aid Bosnia required, most of the troops for the "implementation force" and later the "stabilization force" NATO deployed, and most of the international police. Anyone who doubts the usefulness of NATO and European allies to the United States has not learned from the Balkans experience.

The implementation process was agonizing but at least partly successful, due to a lot of international pressure. Jacques Klein, the American head of the UN's International Police Task Force, mounted a successful scheme to reissue all the license plates, with only the letters common to the Cyrillic and Latin alphabets and no other identifying characteristics, even though they were manufactured in three different parts of the country. Freedom of movement ensued, because no one could tell your ethnicity from your license plates. A 1999 arbitration decision resolved the status of the northeastern town of Brčko, site of some of the war's worst horrors.[38] It belonged, arbitrator Roberts Owen decided, to both the Federation and Republika Srpska, a smokescreen that effectively removed it from both while allowing each to claim victory. American "supervisors" had significant success there as well, while postponing elections entirely for seven years.[39] They had learned that elections in Bosnia, as in many postwar societies, are highly conflictual and tend to increase ethnic division.

But it was clear by 2005, when the Council of Europe's Venice Commission issued a damning report on the Bosnian constitution, that what had been done at Dayton to end the war was inadequate to build a functioning European state.[40] Bosnia needed constitutional reform. That meant revising the Dayton agreements, as the constitution was their mainstay. Don Hays, a former deputy to Ashdown, led the State Department–funded effort at the United States Institute of Peace, with Bosnians representing all the major political parties. Supported by American lawyers from the Public International Law and Policy Group, they discussed amendments to the Dayton constitution intended to reduce its elaborate power-sharing arrangements, make the Bosnian state more functional, and enable it to prepare for EU membership. This was co-optation at its best.

The proposal they produced—later known in a modified version as the "April package"—was less than many hoped for but still a reasonable start at fixing a constitution that had gone too far in enshrining ethnic identity and group rights as the be-all and end-all of Bosnian politics, making the country dysfunctional.[41] The package clarified group, individual, and minority rights as well as mechanisms for protecting the "vital national interests" of Bosnia's constituent peoples. It also included reforms to strengthen the state government and the powers of the prime minister, reduce the presidency's responsibilities, and streamline parliamentary procedures. Most importantly, the amendments included a provision that gave the state government the authority it needed to negotiate and implement the requirements of EU membership. The April package was a down payment on broader reforms that were needed to disentangle the many interlocking vetoes that ensured power sharing immediately after the war but later plagued efforts to govern Bosnia effectively. When it failed by just two votes to gain the two-thirds approval it needed in the Bosnian parliament in 2006, it seemed reasonable to expect it to return the next year and be passed with minor revisions.

That turned out to be wrong. The problem was not the two votes, which belonged to Croats who broke party discipline to vote against the package. It was more serious. Former wartime Prime Minister Haris Silajdžić, whose Bosniak-based party had participated in preparation of the constitutional amendments and had even chaired key meetings, staked his presidential campaign on turning down the April package, which he claimed changed too little and created a loophole that risked leaving Bosnia without a government. When he won the presidency, he refused to reverse himself and took up the cudgels against Republika Srpska leader Milorad Dodik, polarizing Bosnian politics along ethnic lines far more than had been the case in the decade since 1996. Dodik, who had been a relative moderate, began talking about independence and sovereignty for Republika Srpska, Silajdžić denounced its genocidal origins, and the more nationalist Croats revived their idea of the "third entity." Local elites do not always remain co-opted. When one adopts a nationalist narrative, others respond in kind.

Ten years of gradual progress ended in a fit of ethnic nationalist politics. Unhappily, it was just at this moment that the Europeans decided to send a German politician, Christian Schwarz-Schilling, to Bosnia as High Representative. He reflected European thinking that there had been too much international pressure on the Bosnians, especially from the Americans.[42] He wanted to encourage more "local ownership" and put aside the Bonn powers. The April package amendments have never returned for a vote in parliament. Even after the European Court of Human Rights ruled in 2009 against the Bosnian constitution's ethnic criteria for presidential candidates, the political leadership was unable to find a way of fixing the problem, which is easily solved if you are not committed to ethnic nationalism.[43]

Rejection of the April package began a long downhill slide for Bosnia. The Europeans have pushed aside the well-informed and well-meaning High Representatives who succeeded Schwarz-Schilling—Slovak Miroslav Lajčák and Austrian Valentin Inzko—in favor of well-meaning but ineffectual EU representatives committed to local ownership, despite repeated disappointments. The international financial crisis of 2008 stalled Bosnian economic growth, which remained fitful for close to a decade thereafter. The Americans followed the EU lead in agreeing to withdraw international judges and prosecutors from the judiciary and limiting use of the Bonn powers, leaving the High Representative in place but making it impossible for him to use them except in extremis. Only a serious Republika Srpska move to secede or other imminent risk of war would mobilize the kind of international reaction required for the

High Representative to take vigorous action, but it is no longer clear that his decisions would be implemented. The EU representative, who dispenses lots of aid, is now the much more substantial force in Bosnia. But the EU prefers strategic patience—that means waiting for the Bosnians to do the right things—to aggressive action.

The European Commission speaks bluntly about Bosnia's need for a government with the powers needed to negotiate and implement EU membership and has deprived Sarajevo of tens of millions of euros because it has refused to reform, but at the same time it has sent new funds, and also offered Bosnia a shortcut to EU candidacy status, provided the country adopts labor market and other reforms.[44] These are slowly making their way through various parliaments and the many levels of government required to enact them. The EU has also accepted a "coordination mechanism" that gives not only the entities but even the cantons within the Federation veto power. Implementation therefore lags and Bosnians remain essentially deadlocked on many important issues.[45] Frustrated in their dealings with the Sarajevo government, the Europeans increasingly deal directly with the Republika Srpska government in Banja Luka, thus increasing its prominence and encouraging separatist inclinations.[46]

The results have been underwhelming. Dayton ended a war but failed to provide an adequate foundation for a warm peace or functional governance. Its constitutional power-sharing provisions ensure that ethnically based political parties govern and exploit a captured state and publicly owned companies for the benefit of their leaders.[47] Corruption, cronyism, fake privatizations, and political appointments to public service positions, including the courts, are the rule rather than the exception. Hundreds of millions of dollars have been siphoned out of public companies into private pockets. More than ten years after failure of the April package, Bosnia is mired in ethnic nationalist polarization, even though Silajdžić has left the political scene. Repeated attempts at constitutional reform have failed. Dodik, still a political force, remains resistant, though American imposition of personal travel and financial sanctions against him has made him marginally more pliable than at times in the past. He has backed off scheduling referenda on the authority of the constitutional court and on Republika Srpska independence, but he is arming his police for war with Russian assistance.[48]

Today's Bosnia is a caricature of wartime Bosnia. Most of the Bosniak and Serb leaders make political hay by railing against each other.

Nationalist Croats shift allegiance from side to side, depending on who is making the better offer, which is what they did during the war, especially in Mostar. More nationalist Croats also seek a "third entity," which would amount to a revival of Herzeg-Bosna, the wartime Croat parastate. Their most recent scheme in this regard is an effort at electoral reform that would reduce the electoral weight of Croats who live in Bosniak-majority cantons.[49] The third entity was a bad idea at Dayton, when the Croats controlled arms flow into the Federation and contributed substantially to the Federation effort. Nor is it a good idea more than twenty years later. Creation of a Croat entity would necessarily result in formation of a land-locked, isolated, and likely radicalized Muslim entity (or two) in central Bosnia. Neither Croatia nor Serbia would like that.

The rest of the world would not either, but the internationals are also a shadow of their former selves, with the important exception of the Russians. The Americans lean toward the Bosniaks and strengthening the state government while weakening the group rights protected so strongly in the Dayton constitution. Belittling whatever initiative the Americans undertake, the Europeans have lowered the bar to begin accession talks in the hope that getting Bosnia into the membership process will fix everything. Turkey tries, with only occasional success, to play honest broker, though President Erdoğan's turn toward authoritarianism and Islamism has made him far chummier with the Bosniak member of the presidency, Bakir Izetbegović, the son of wartime leader Alija Izetbegović. The Russians support the Serbs and maximum autonomy for Republika Srpska, not the least to ensure that Bosnia never tries to enter NATO. Moscow is arming and training Republika Srpska's police far beyond the levels required to deal with the normal law-and-order problems arising in the entity.[50]

Little is solved, because Bosnia has a constitution that makes it difficult to solve anything without all three ethnic groups agreeing. There is little incentive for that to happen. Politicians who appeal across ethnic lines rarely win elections. When they do succeed, the ethnic nationalists from all three "constituent" peoples try to write new rules of the game to prevent a repetition. Their highly centralized political parties control patronage and jobs in public-sector companies. The country continues to claim to prepare for EU membership and even managed in 2010 to meet the requirements for visa-free travel to the Schengen Area. But it falls farther and farther behind the competition in the regatta to join the EU.

Milorad Dodik visits Moscow frequently, stuffs his bank accounts with rubles, and jabbers about independence and sovereignty. It is not going to happen. Not even Serbia would recognize an independent Republika Srpska, much less incorporate it into Serbia, because that would end Belgrade's own hopes for EU membership.

Some Bosnian Croats insist on their own, ethnically defined entity. That is not going to happen either.[51] The Bosnian Croats got a good deal at Dayton. If they have been unsuccessful at parlaying their constitutional position into real power, that is their problem, not anyone else's. They certainly should not get a better deal now that the war is over and the Herzegovinian stranglehold on access to central Bosnia has been broken.

Where does the solution lie? How can Bosnia's governance be unblocked and become more functional? Some hope it might come from the country's citizens.[52] Dysfunctional and corrupt governance generated widespread protests and street-organized "plenums" in the winter and spring of 2014, forcing the resignations of some cantonal governments. The protests had the great virtue of raising issues that transcend ethnic divisions, even if they occurred mainly in Bosniak-majority areas of the Federation (due in part to repression in Republika Srpska). Nationalist Croat, Serb, and Bosniak politicians all tried to cast the protests as ethnically menacing, though they arguably demonstrated that Bosnian citizens of all ethnic groups want improved and less ethnically focused governance based on the creation of a "supra-ethnic citizenship identity of their participants" and a "'secure space' for participatory democracy."[53]

October 2014 elections were nevertheless inconclusive; the October 2018 polls were no more definitive. Modest shifts away from the ethnic nationalists have not yet deprived them of their decisive weight in parliament and in the two entities. Some hope for reform from the municipal level, where citizens can more easily turn out those politicians who do not produce benefits.[54] Direct election of mayors, which Bosnia adopted in 2004, improved performance at that level, where issues-based, rather than ethnicity-based, politics are easier to pursue. Local government also has the virtue of allowing broader access to power, since numerical minorities are often majorities in some localities. Decentralization thereby shares power more broadly, without ethnic criteria and vetoes. But it can also be harder to find capable people and uncorrupted institutions.

A lot now depends on the EU, especially Germany, the UK, and Croatia. If Angela Merkel were to do for Bosnia what we shall see she did eventually for Serbia—telling Bosnian leaders in clear terms what they need to do to make their candidacy for the EU a reality—that would help a great deal. The "reform" initiative in the fall of 2014 by London and Berlin fell far short of that. It may have merit, but it is unlikely to make a big political difference unless the international community does what is necessary to prevent crony privatizations. It would help if Zagreb, as it has done sometimes in the past, were to read the Bosnian Croats the riot act, telling them that their best bet is to use the one-third of the state that they gained at Dayton to strengthen Bosnia's governance and help it prepare for EU membership. But Croat ethnic nationalism, including in Zagreb, has grown more virulent in recent years, not less.

Many Bosnians, especially Bosniaks, look to the United States to do something, including deployment of U.S. troops. But the interventionist moment is over. Washington is worried about many other things and is not going to save Bosnia, unless its sovereignty or territorial integrity is seriously threatened. Washington wants Brussels to do the heavy lifting. There is not, in any event, a lot the Americans can do beyond trying to accelerate the reforms the EU is demanding, though helping the Bosnians to take another look at the April package and constitutional reform would also be a good idea. Bosnians need to look to themselves, to each other, to make a future that is better than their present.

Bosnia today is an unhappy place, but for the most part it is not a deadly one, and certainly not a genocidal one. Inter-ethnic violence is rare. Only a single American peacekeeper was killed in Bosnia after the war, despite many challenges.[55] A few hundred European troops remain in the country, spread around in militarily insignificant units. The economy needs reform and the society needs greater ethnic integration. Democracy provides lots of opportunity for change, but citizens need to exercise their options to get it. If they don't, that is for them to decide. That is democracy too.

Could this persistently unhappy place return to war? Reversion of that sort happens in many countries. There is no ruling it out completely in Bosnia. But any future war there will be different from the 1990s episode. Yugoslavia is no longer falling apart. Milošević is gone. Politicians are still stoking ethnic tensions, which Dayton did little to attenuate. But the neighboring states are both more consolidated and more constrained now than they were then. While nationalist ambitions for Greater Serbia still reverberate, the nationalists who govern in Belgrade today have European aspirations that limit their appetite for intervention. As a member of both the EU and NATO, Croatia would likewise be under enormous pressure not to intervene in a new Bosnian war. The Sarajevo government has at its disposal, at least in theory, a small but well-trained and unified army. In the event of renewed fighting, its loyal components would likely be ordered to seize Brčko, which is the keystone of Republika Srpska. The outcome would depend on a likely days-long battle there.

Preventing such a scenario should be topmost on European and American minds. The Europeans should concentrate their troops in Brčko, where they would be a meaningful bulwark against both Republika Srpska independence and any effort to split the entity at its most vulnerable point. Britain added a few troops to the EU contingent in Bosnia in anticipation of the October 2018 elections, which generated political tension. Pleas for the United States to follow suit, or even to establish a permanent base in Bosnia, are likely to go unheard unless things get worse, because of commitments elsewhere.[56]

But things could get worse. Russia may be inclined to try its hand at destabilizing Bosnia by supporting Republika Srpska's independence ambitions. Dodik has been ready and willing to act as Moscow's agent, in return for political and financial support. Republika Srpska might join the Russian vassals in Georgia (South Ossetia and Abkhazia), Moldova (Transnistria), and Ukraine (Crimea, Donetsk, and Luhansk) as thorns in the side of the West that distract the respective suzerains from pursuing membership in NATO and the EU. This is an outcome Washington and Brussels need to work assiduously to avoid. How to do so is discussed in Chapter 6.

Notes

1. Andrew Wachtel and Christopher Bennett, "The Dissolution of Yugoslavia," in *Confronting the Yugoslav Controversies: A Scholars' Initiative*, ed. Charles W. Ingrao and Thomas A. Emmert (West Lafayette, IN: Purdue University Press, 2009), 13–47.
2. Louis Sell, *Slobodan Milošević and the Destruction of Yugoslavia* (Durham: Duke University Press, 2002), 170.
3. Karl Mueller, "The Demise of Yugoslavia and the Destruction of Bosnia: Strategic Causes, Effects, and Responses," in *Deliberate Force: A Case*

Study in Effective Air Campaigning: Final Report of the Air University Balkans Air Campaign Study, ed. Robert C. Owen (Maxwell AFB, AL: Air University Press, 2000), 10, http://www.au.af.mil/au/awc/awcgate/au/owen.pdf.
4. Anto Knežević, "Alija Izetbegović's 'Islamic Declaration': Its Substance and Its Western Reception," Islamic Studies 36, nos. 2/3 (1997): 483–521, http://www.jstor.org/stable/23076209.
5. Gale Stokes, "Independence and the Fate of Minorities, 1991–1992," in Ingrao and Emmert, Confronting the Yugoslav Controversies, 83–112.
6. Richard Caplan, Europe and the Recognition of New States in Yugoslavia (Cambridge: Cambridge University Press, 2005).
7. "The Conflicts," International Criminal Tribunal for the Former Yugoslavia, http://www.icty.org/en/about/what-former-yugoslavia/conflicts.
8. The failure of these efforts is discussed extensively by James E. Goodby in "When War Won Out: Bosnian Peace Plans before Dayton," International Negotiation 1, no. 3 (1996): 501–23.
9. Josip Glaurdić, The Hour of Europe: Western Powers and the Breakup of Yugoslavia (New Haven: Yale University Press, 2011).
10. Matjaž Klemenčič, "The International Community and the FRY/Belligerents, 1989–1997," in Ingrao Emmert, Confronting the Yugoslav Controversies, 177–80.
11. Marko Attila Hoare, How Bosnia Armed (London: Saqi Books, 2004).
12. John Pomfret and David B. Ottaway, "U.S. Allies' Arms Aid to Bosnia Detailed," Los Angeles Times, May 12, 1996, http://articles.latimes.com/1996-05-12/news/mn-3437_1_arms-smuggling.
13. Adrian Shtuni, "The Western Balkans: A Jihadist Pipeline to Syria and Iraq," Fikra Forum, January 29, 2015.
14. Richard C. Holbrooke, To End a War (New York: Random House, 1998), 296.
15. My role in making the Bosnian Federation real is recounted in Daniel Serwer, "A Bosnian Federation Memoir," in Herding Cats: Multiparty Mediation in a Complex World, ed. Chester A. Crocker, Fen Osler Hampson, and Pamela R. Aall (Washington, DC: United States Institute of Peace Press, 1999), 547–86.
16. Derek Chollet, The Road to the Dayton Accords: A Study of American Statecraft (New York: Palgrave Macmillan, 2005).
17. Tim Ripley, Operation Deliberate Force: The UN and NATO Campaign in Bosnia 1995 (Lancaster, UK: Centre for Defence and International Security Studies, 1999), 268.
18. For a compelling statement of this perspective, see Peter W. Galbraith, "Washington, Erdut and Dayton: Negotiating and Implementing Peace in Croatia and Bosnia-Herzegovina," Cornell International Law Journal

30, no. 3 (1997): 643–49, https://scholarship.law.cornell.edu/cgi/viewcontent.cgi?referer=https://www.bing.com/&httpsredir=1&article=1408&context=cilj.
19. Holbrooke, *To End a War*, 197.
20. I discussed some of the issues treated here in "Dayton Reexamined," *Axess Magasin*, June 2013, 25–27.
21. AmEmbassy Belgrade 2419 to SecState, May 19, 1995, paragraph 4, https://www.peacefare.net/state-department-belgrade-cables-1995/.
22. Sell, *Milošević and the Destruction of Yugoslavia*, 216.
23. Adam LeBor, *Milošević: A Biography* (New Haven: Yale University Press, 2004), 245.
24. AmEmbassy Belgrade 823 to SecState, February 17, 1995, paragraph 5, https://www.peacefare.net/state-department-belgrade-cables-1995/.
25. Sell, *Milošević and the Destruction of Yugoslavia*, 245.
26. AmEmbassy Belgrade 2468 to SecState, May 22, 1995, https://www.peacefare.net/state-department-belgrade-cables-1995/; LeBor, *Milošević*, 246.
27. Daniel W. Drezner, *The Sanctions Paradox: Economic Statecraft and International Relations* (Cambridge: Cambridge University Press, 2000).
28. Agency for Statistics of Bosnia and Herzegovina, "Cenzus [sic] of Population, Households and Dwellings in Bosnia and Herzegovina, 2013: Final Results," Sarajevo, June 2016, http://www.popis2013.ba/popis2013/doc/Popis2013prvoIzdanje.pdf.
29. Private conversation with the author at Dayton in November 1995.
30. Holbrooke, *To End a War*, 309.
31. James Kennedy and Liliana Riga, "A Liberal Route from Homogeneity? US Policymakers and the Liberalization of Ethnic Nationalists in Bosnia's Dayton Accords," *Nationalism and Ethnic Politics* 19, no. 2 (2013): 163–86, https://www.tandfonline.com/doi/abs/10.1080/13537113.2013.788910?journalCode=fnep20.
32. The author heard this from an American official present at the time.
33. Barbara F. Walter, *Committing to Peace: The Successful Settlement of Civil Wars* (Princeton: Princeton University Press, 2002).
34. Steven L. Burg and Paul S. Shoup, *The War in Bosnia-Herzegovina: Ethnic Conflict and International Intervention* (Armonk, NY: M. E. Sharpe, 1999), 172.
35. The initial shortcomings, especially the compromises with ethnic nationalism, were apparent at the time. See Jane M.O. Sharp, "Dayton Report Card," *International Security* 22, no. 3 (Winter 1996/98): 101–37, and somewhat later, Richard Caplan, "Assessing the Dayton Accord: The Structural Weaknesses of the General Framework Agreement for Peace in Bosnia and Herzegovina," *Diplomacy and Statecraft* 11, no. 2 (July 2000): 213–32.

36. Oscar Vera and Karmen Fields, "Bosnia-Herzegovina: The Third Entity Movement," in *Criminalized Power Structures: The Overlooked Enemies of Peace*, ed. Michael Dziedzi (Lanham, MD: Rowman & Littlefield, 2016), 27–51.
37. "GNI per Capita, Atlas Method, Bosnia and Herzegovina (1996–2016)," *The World Bank*, 2016, https://data.worldbank.org/indicator/NY.GNP.PCAP.CD?locations=BA.
38. "Secretary-General Strongly Endorses Decision to Create Brčko District of Bosnia and Herzegovina: Meetings Coverage and Press Releases," United Nations, March 1999, https://www.un.org/press/en/1999/19990305.sgsm6917.html.
39. Robert William Farrand and Allison Frendak-Blume, *Reconstruction and Peace Building in the Balkans: The Brčko Experience* (Lanham, MD: Rowman & Littlefield, 2011).
40. European Commission for Democracy through Law (Venice Commission), *Opinion on the Constitutional Situation in Bosnia and Herzegovina and the Powers of the High Representative*, March 11, 2005, http://www.venice.coe.int/webforms/documents/default.aspx?pdffile=CDL-AD(2005)004-e.
41. Don Hays and Jason Crosby, *From Dayton to Brussels: Constitutional Preparations for Bosnia's EU Accession* (Washington, DC: United States Institute of Peace Press, 2006), https://www.usip.org/publications/2006/10/dayton-brussels-constitutional-preparations-bosnias-eu-accession.
42. Gerald Knaus and Felix Martin, "Lessons from Bosnia and Herzegovina: Travails of the European Raj," *Journal of Democracy* 18, no. 5 (2003): 60–74, https://www.journalofdemocracy.org/article/lessons-bosnia-and-herzegovina-travails-european-raj.
43. Judgment delivered by a Grand Chamber, *Sejdić and Finci v. Bosnia and Herzegovina*, nos. 27796/06 and 34836/06, ECHR (2009), https://www.opensocietyfoundations.org/sites/default/files/grand-chamber-judgment-20091222.pdf.
44. Frank-Walter Steinmeier and Philip Hammond to Federica Mogherini and Johannes Hahn, Berlin/London, November 4, 2014, http://infographics.economist.com/20141108_Letter/Letter.pdf.
45. Bobo Weber, "Substantial Change on the Horizon? A Monitoring Report on the EU's New Bosnia and Herzegovina Initiative," *Democratization Policy Council* (Berlin-Sarajevo, March 2017), https://ba.boell.org/bs/2017/04/03/substantial-change-horizon-monitoring-report-eus-new-bosnia-and-herzegovina-initiative.
46. Some even propose separate EU accession for Republika Srpska: Doğa Ulaş Eralp, *Politics of the European Union in Bosnia-Herzegovina: Between Conflict and Democracy* (Lanham, MD: Lexington Books, 2012).

47. Srdjan Blagovcanin and Boris Divjak, *How Bosnia's Political Economy Holds It Back and What to Do About It* (Washington, DC: Center for Transatlantic Relations, Johns Hopkins School of Advanced International Studies, 2015), https://www.peacefare.net/wp-content/uploads/2015/08/Blagovcanin-and-Divjak_final.pdf.
48. Reuf Bajrovic, Raichard Kraemer, and Emir Suljagic, "Bosnia on the Russian Chopping Block: The Potential for Violence and Steps to Prevent It," Foreign Policy Research Institute, March 2018, https://www.fpri.org/article/2018/03/bosnia-russian-chopping-block-potential-violence-steps-prevent/.
49. Zeljana Zovko, "Wanted: Even-Handed US Engagement in Bosnia and Herzegovina," The Atlantic Council, February 2018, http://www.atlanticcouncil.org/blogs/new-atlanticist/wanted-even-handed-us-engagement-in-bosnia-and-herzegovina.
50. Reuf Bajrovic, Raichard Kraemer, and Emir Suljagic, "Bosnia on the Russian Chopping Block: The Potential for Violence and Steps to Prevent It," Foreign Policy Research Institute, March 2018, https://www.fpri.org/article/2018/03/bosnia-russian-chopping-block-potential-violence-steps-prevent/.
51. Daniel Serwer, "Bosnia Needs to Get Boring," *Peacefare.net*, October 12, 2014, https://www.peacefare.net/2014/10/12/.
52. Jasmin Mujanović, *Hunger and Fury the Crisis of Democracy in the Balkans* (London: Hurst, 2018).
53. Nina Belyaeva, "Citizen Plenums in Bosnia Protests: Creating a Post-ethnic Identity," in *Non-Western Social Movements and Participatory Democracy*, ed. Ekim Arbatli and Diana Rosenberg (Cham: Springer, 2017), 115–38.
54. "Municipalization: A Popular Governance Model for Bosnia and Herzegovina, Revised Model," Coalition 143 (K-143), June 24, 2014, https://www.scribd.com/document/231194321/K-143-Municipalization-Model-FULL-document-ENG.
55. Center for Military History, "Bosnia-Herzegovina: The U.S. Army's Role in Peace Enforcement Operations 1995–2004," CMH Pub 70-97-1, https://history.army.mil/html/books/070/70-97-1/cmhPub_70-97-1.pdf.
56. Damir Marusic, Sarah Bedenbaugh, and Damon Wilson, "Balkans Forward: New US Strategy for the Region," The Atlantic Council, November 2017, http://www.atlanticcouncil.org/images/Balkans_Forward_web_1128.pdf.

Open Access This chapter is distributed under the terms of the Creative Commons Attribution 4.0 International License (http://creativecommons.org/licenses/by/4.0/), which permits use, duplication, adaptation, distribution and reproduction in any medium or format, as long as you give appropriate credit to the original author(s) and the source, a link is provided to the Creative Commons license and any changes made are indicated.

The images or other third party material in this chapter are included in the work's Creative Commons license, unless indicated otherwise in the credit line; if such material is not included in the work's Creative Commons license and the respective action is not permitted by statutory regulation, users will need to obtain permission from the license holder to duplicate, adapt or reproduce the material.

CHAPTER 4

Macedonia: Timely Prevention Works

Abstract Three drivers led to war in Bosnia: breakup of Yugoslavia, Milošević's political ambitions and military capabilities, and ethnic nationalism. The first of these affected Macedonia. The other two were attenuated. Macedonia has mostly avoided war and made significant economic progress, with help from the UN, the EU, and the United States as well as decentralization and power sharing between Macedonians and Albanians. Greece's refusal to accept Macedonia's name, however, has stalled entry into NATO, slowed progress toward the EU, and aggravated ethnic tensions. A now agreed solution to the "name" issue would be a major gain for Macedonia and the region, if implemented in both countries. The door will then open for the "Republic of North Macedonia" to enter NATO and begin EU accession talks.

Keywords Conflict prevention · "Name" issue · Ohrid Framework Agreement · "Northern Macedonia"

Today's Macedonia owes its distinct and separate existence as a political entity to Socialist Yugoslavia. During the Yugoslav monarchy between the world wars, what is now Macedonia was initially the *banovina* (province) of Southern Serbia, which became Vardar Banovina in 1929. It was only after World War II that the Yugoslav Republic of Macedonia came into existence. In Tito's way of thinking, Macedonian identity—based

© The Author(s) 2019
D. Serwer, *From War to Peace in the Balkans, the Middle East and Ukraine*, Palgrave Critical Studies in Post-Conflict Recovery, https://doi.org/10.1007/978-3-030-02173-3_4

on language, history, and religion—was useful because it fended off both Bulgarian territorial and Serbian identity claims. The modern Macedonians are, however, Slavs, not Greeks. Their language is Slavic and related to Bulgarian, but distinct from Serbo-Croatian (now termed Serbian, Croatian, Montenegrin, or Bosnian, depending on whom you are talking to). Whatever antecedents existed for Macedonian identity, it is hard to picture how a Macedonian state would have emerged when it did without a big boost from Socialist Yugoslavia.

But Macedonia has never been all ethnically Macedonian. There is a reason the French and Italians call a mixed-fruit salad a *macédoine/macedonia*. The numerically largest minority is Albanian, about one-quarter of the population. Mother Teresa is the best-known Albanian from what is today Macedonia (born in Skopje in 1910). Ten percent are Turks, Roma, Serbs, Bosniaks, and other Yugoslavs as well as Vlachs and Bulgarians. The country is thoroughly mixed ethnically, even if the Albanian population is concentrated in the northwest and in the capital, Skopje (*Shkup* in Albanian). Some Albanians in Macedonia would have preferred to be part of a majority in Kosovo or Albania. Some of its Serbs would have preferred to be part of the majority in Serbia. Its Bulgarians—as well as Greek neighbors and others in the Balkans— have often viewed Macedonia and its language as nothing more than an offshoot of Bulgaria and Bulgarian. It is not easy to be an ethnically mixed country in the Balkans, especially when your northern neighbors (majority-Albanian Kosovo and majority-Slavic Serbia) are fighting and your two largest populations speak mutually incomprehensible mother tongues.

So the dissolution of Yugoslavia certainly put Macedonia at risk. The centrifugal forces were strong. When Slovenia and Croatia left the Yugoslav Federation in 1991, Macedonia had to follow or risk being left in a Serb-dominated Federation. It held a referendum in September 1991 that was approved by 99% of the 72% of registered voters who went to the polls. Most Albanians and Serbs boycotted. Albanians disliked the idea of independence because it would separate them from their compatriots in Kosovo. Pristina and its university were historical, cultural, and intellectual centers of Albanian nationalism. Albanians in Macedonia had easy communication with Albanians in Kosovo during the Socialist period, when the boundary was invisible and porous, like the boundary between Virginia and Maryland (or today France and Germany). Independence inserted an international border between branches of Albanian families. Serbs likewise disliked Macedonian independence because it would separate them from Serbia and weaken whatever Serb-dominated state emerged from Socialist Yugoslavia.

Why did war not follow? The other ingredients were diluted, and the international community was far more proactive.[1] Serbian nationalism had nowhere near the same significance in Macedonia as it had in Bosnia. Serbs officially represented only 2% of the population in the last Socialist census, and Macedonian identity was strongly felt by more than 65% of the population.[2] Milošević was preoccupied with Croatia and Bosnia, both of which had larger percentages of Serbs. He had already abandoned the effort to hold on to Slovenia, where few Serbs lived. He withdrew the Yugoslav National Army from Macedonia without shots fired in February 1992. Leaving Macedonia with a weak army based on its Yugoslav territorial reserve forces (a home guard), it represented no threat and would be easy pickings later, if Milošević so desired. Neither his political ambitions nor Serbian nationalism were immediately at stake.

Macedonian President Kiro Gligorov in November 1992 requested UN observers to ensure his country's territorial integrity. His immediate concern was the possible impact of fighting elsewhere in former Yugoslavia, especially an influx of refugees from Kosovo that might trigger Albanian and Serbian intervention, as well as Turkish and Greek responses. Macedonia was not yet a UN member. Gligorov, acutely aware of his country's need for international recognition, wanted to protect its sovereignty and independence, increase its diplomatic profile, and prevent war from spreading into its territory.[3] An international peacekeeping force would serve all these purposes, even if the conventional military threat proved minimal.

Lucky Macedonia not only got the UN's first explicitly preventive deployment, UNPREDEP, but also benefited from Nordic and eventually U.S. troops, who were sent as a token by President Bill Clinton because Macedonia was relatively safe for peacekeepers compared to Croatia and Bosnia, where European observers were already under fire. UNPREDEP stayed in Macedonia until early 1999, working hard but somewhat surreptitiously to solidify the country internally as well as to observe and report on external threats, including those arising from the breakdown of law and order in Albania during 1996 and 1997 and in Kosovo in 1998 and 1999. The UN mission was withdrawn due to a Chinese veto in the UN Security Council after Macedonia, in an ill-fated move meant to attract investment, recognized and established diplomatic relations with Taiwan, shortly before the long-feared outflow of Albanian refugees from Kosovo actually began.

While Gligorov's worst fears did not materialize, one neighbor did peacefully but energetically contest one aspect of Macedonian statehood, the country's name, at independence and for more than twenty-five years thereafter. Greece claimed the exclusive right to the label "Macedonia" for one of its provinces. Athens also asserted that Skopje's use of it entailed a claim on Greek territory. The authorities in Skopje have not asserted such a claim, and the third article in the country's constitution, adopted to satisfy Athens, precludes one: "The Republic of Macedonia has no territorial pretensions towards any neighboring state."[4] Macedonia also changed its flag and deleted numerical estimates of the Macedonian minority in Greece from its foreign ministry website to please Athens, all to no avail.[5] Macedonia in any event is far too weak militarily to represent a threat to Greece, which Skopje would prefer to have as a NATO ally rather than an adversary.

When asked for evidence of Macedonian irredentism, Greeks routinely whip out a photograph showing a map allegedly displayed in Macedonian schoolrooms that depicts the Macedonian flag blanketing not only Macedonia's sovereign territory but also Greece's northern provinces. Macedonians claim this is a depiction of the extent of ethnic Macedonian presence, not a claim to territory. But that is little comfort to Greeks, who are loath to admit the existence of minorities within their own population and claim that "Macedonia," a name associated with more than twelve hundred places in the United States, belongs exclusively to Greece and its supposedly pure Hellenic tradition, traced back without interruption to the ancients.

Skopje was nevertheless admitted to the United Nations as The Former Yugoslav Republic of Macedonia (The FYROM: alphabetized in the General Assembly under "T") in 1993, a temporary expedient that Greece agreed in 1995 could be used in other international bodies as well.[6] The United Nations, mostly in the person of American lawyer Matthew Nimitz, tried for the next twenty-five years to resolve the "name" issue. As special representative of the UN secretary-general, Nimitz shuttled between Athens and Skopje, occasionally convening the parties for a discussion of proposals. The Greeks wanted a new constitutional name without "Macedonia" that would have to be used for all purposes (*erga omnes* is the Latin term of art). The Macedonians wanted one that could be readily shortened to "Macedonia," which they intend to keep using. The dispute proved intractable, because like so many other Balkan issues it pitted one ethnic identity and nationalism, Greek, against another, Macedonian.

Greek preoccupation with the name issue is rooted in Athens's own attitude toward minorities within Greece, as it denies they exist, and related claims about Greek identity. Coached by nationalist politicians, many Greeks want to believe that they are descended directly from the ancient Greeks and have exclusive rights to that distinction. Anyone who knows the history of barbarian and Slavic invasions as well as the consequent mixing of gene pools should have doubts about that claim. The population of Athens was fewer than 10,000 in 1800.[7] It had been closer to 250,000 in the fifth century BC and is now more than 650,000. What likelihood is there that today's Greek population is all descended from the ancient Greeks? Greek nationalism, and the claim to inheritance of ancient genes and culture, is not continuous but—like Serbian and Albanian nationalism—a product of the nineteenth century, specifically the romantic awakening associated with the British poet Lord Byron, who died in Greece after fighting for its independence from the Ottomans.

Whatever its origins, the consequences of the name issue were pernicious. Greece's former Prime Minister Antonis Samaras went so far as to say that he wanted to see the dissolution of Macedonia and the formation of a Greater Albania, rather than accept a solution that included "Macedonia."[8] Some Macedonians do claim to be descended from the ancient Greeks, and their past leadership, in particular Prime Minister Nikola Gruevski, touted that connection, but most realize that neither genetic nor cultural lineage is likely, especially as their language is Slavic.[9] President Gligorov in the 1990s used to explicitly deny any connection to the ancient Macedonians.

While the name issue remained an irritant for more than twenty-five years, the bigger immediate threat to the Macedonian state at independence did not come from Greece, which became an important investor and trading partner despite its hostility to the name "Macedonia." The threat came initially from inside the country. At independence, Albanians were 21.7% of the population. Their members of parliament abstained from voting on the new constitution, which treated the new state as belonging to "the Macedonian people." Only gradually did Albanians in Macedonia begin to participate actively in governing the country. Today an unwritten but so far inviolate power-sharing rule requires that one of their larger vote-getting parties join the government and be given substantial portfolios. The Albanians do not object to calling the country "Macedonia," but they want to see the name issue resolved to enable NATO membership, which they view as a guarantee of the democratic future of the country and its willingness to protect its non-Macedonian citizens.

The "Albanian question"—that is, whether the Albanians will live in many countries or in just one Greater Albania—has arisen repeatedly in the more than twenty-five years of Macedonia's independence. It became acute in 1999. Macedonia received about 350,000 Kosovo Albanian refugees chased out by Serb forces during March, April, and May of that year, well over 10% of the Macedonia's population. The influx significantly increased the number of Macedonia's Albanian inhabitants and threatened to destabilize a still weak state. Nevertheless, Gligorov's nightmare scenario of Albanian, Serbian, Greek, and Bulgarian involvement, often repeated by Richard Holbrooke, never materialized, in part because the warnings mobilized American and European diplomats to effective prevention. The peacekeepers were gone, but Macedonia managed the crisis effectively, with a great deal of international assistance.[10]

It was not the Albanian refugee influx during the Kosovo War that put Macedonia at serious risk. In June 1999 the Kosovar refugees returned rapidly as soon as Serbian forces withdrew. They left behind a still weak state, one that had not yet done much to convince its Albanian population that it would be treated well enough to offset the losses from separation from Albanians in Kosovo.

The full story of the Albanian rebellion in Macedonia in 2001 has not been told.[11] The insurgency was fed from southern Serbia and Kosovo, in part by Albanians who had not done well politically in Kosovo's first postwar elections and were seeking other outlets. But there were real grievances inside Macedonia as well. Though Albanian political parties had begun to participate in Macedonian governments, Albanians still felt that they were being treated like second-class citizens. They sought official recognition of their language, which is a vital dimension of Albanian identity, and of the multilingual University of Tetovo, established in 1994, as well as permission to use the ethnic Albanian flag (which also doubles as the flag of Albania). They sought equality in the Macedonian administration and army. They wanted decentralization that would allow municipalities, some of which had Albanian majorities, more self-governance.

The Albanians in Macedonia did not, however, seek to destroy the Macedonian state or open the door to union with Kosovo or Albania. Doing so would have put at risk Kosovo's still unfulfilled ambitions for independence. It would also have meant a thoroughly unsatisfactory territorial outcome. Macedonian Prime Minister Ljubčo Georgievski was open to partition of his country and even had the Macedonian Academy write an imitation of the Serbian Academy memorandum that had propounded nationalist goals.[12] But he was unwilling to give up an inch of Skopje, which held the largest concentration of Albanians in the country. Nor did most Albanians in Macedonia want to open a Pandora's box, precipitating a series of partitions in Kosovo and Bosnia and destabilizing much of the Balkans. The 2001 Albanian rebellion was a violent one, but its militants accepted the territorial status quo and sought expanded Albanian political participation and rights within the existing state structure.

The seven months or so of conflict in 2001 did not end with a much-violated NATO-negotiated cease-fire but rather with signing of the Ohrid Framework Agreement, which provided Albanians in Macedonia with the promise of a stronger role in state institutions, more use of their language, and serious devolution of power to the municipal level.[13] The basic ideas in the agreement had been put forward months earlier by Robert Frowick, the American head of the Organization for Security and Cooperation in Europe mission in Macedonia. European and American negotiators collaborated in mediating the negotiations and in developing the formal agreement, signed in August 2001. The National Liberation Army (NLA), which had conducted the rebellion, agreed to demilitarize, disarm, and reintegrate. It reemerged under its surprisingly mild-mannered commander, Ali Ahmeti, as the Democratic Union for Integration, which has outpolled its Albanian rivals while participating in Macedonian governments since 2002.

This is an instance of relatively early international engagement, mainly of a political sort but with NATO military power looming in the distance. The Macedonian government and the NLA were both ready to end the fighting, as neither had much capacity to escalate further without causing the Europeans and Americans to respond in ways that would hurt their respective causes. The Ohrid Agreement was a mutually enticing opportunity at a moment of mutually hurting stalemate, as it preserved the Macedonian state while guaranteeing Albanians a strong role within it. Macedonia might well have exploded in 2001 under pressure from Albanian nationalism, with catastrophic consequences for the Balkans and beyond. Prevention and early diplomatic intervention worked once again, because the ethnic nationalism was relatively attenuated and not associated with a clearly defined territory, military capabilities were limited, and political ambitions were restrained. Without Milošević's and Serbia's involvement, the fighting was blessedly brief and contained in the north, with combat deaths well below the 1000 victims that usually qualify as a war.

The history of Macedonia since then resembles Macedonia's folk dance, the *oro*: three steps forward, two steps back. It includes progress followed by deterioration on both the domestic and the international fronts. The progress on the domestic front is of two sorts: implementation of the Ohrid Agreement and improvement in the country's economic prospects.

The record on the Ohrid Agreement is modestly positive on decentralization, Albanian representation in state institutions, parliamentary safeguards, university education, language, and ethnic symbols.[14] Ethnic Macedonians think Albanians should be satisfied, but they are not.[15] As the American embassy put it: Ohrid "is still an effective tool to reduce the risk of another civil conflict, even though implementation has been a 'mixed bag.'"[16]

The Albanians would like official use of their language by the Skopje government throughout the entire country as well as more fiscal decentralization to the municipal level than provided for in the original agreement. Some Macedonians resist, fearing a weakened "binational" state. A law regulating language use passed the parliament twice by early 2018, but President Gjorge Ivanov refused to sign it. The lack of taxation authority at the local level limits resources and local autonomy (and likely also patronage and corruption). Issues of this sort exist throughout much of Europe and in the United States. It might even be said that they are perpetual. Though subsidiarity (handling of issues at the lowest effective level) is by now a well-established principle in Europe, it is implemented in widely varying ways throughout the EU.[17] The variations in municipal and other local government structures and powers are even greater in the United States.

Many of the other remaining issues concern the degree to which legislation has been implemented, in the spirit as well as the letter of the law. Years more will be required in Macedonia, even if things are moving generally in the right direction. Any faster pace might risk a backlash among Macedonians, some of whom treat every Albanian advance as their loss. In 2011, at the tenth-anniversary celebration of the Ohrid Agreement, the only major Macedonian politician to appear was the young foreign minister, Nikola Poposki. He made it clear he thought the Ohrid Agreement had saved his country, but precious few of his Macedonian colleagues would say it out loud. The agreement has not transformed relations between Macedonians and Albanians, even if it has relieved the most acute grievances felt on the Albanian side. Prevention has allowed a good deal of practical cooperation between Macedonians and Albanians, but it has not done a lot to break down their tradition of living separate, parallel lives.[18]

The other sense in which Macedonia has progressed is economic. During the first decade after independence, the sclerotic state-dominated economy had been held back by Greek hostility, painful privatizations, and the wars both farther north and in Macedonia itself. Macedonians used to complain bitterly about the small Albanian family-owned companies that paid few taxes and ignored the many regulations left over from the country's Socialist past. Many Macedonians in the 1990s were committed to large, non-competitive, state-owned enterprises left over from Socialist Yugoslavia. Few of those have survived.

There was virtue in the Albanian example. Skopje eventually began to encourage entrepreneurial success. Made an EU candidate country in 2005, it lowered tax rates and streamlined regulations. The Macedonian economy is now rated the freest in the region.[19] The government and citizens have also discovered that they can borrow, leading to large increases in public and private debt. The results have been dramatic. The economy stagnated for the decade after independence. Since 2001, GDP has tripled, despite near-recession in 2009 and 2010 due to the European recession, as well as declines in 2012 and 2015. That is a substantial peace dividend, even if it has not been shared equitably across the society.

There is one important but largely invisible international achievement in recent years for Macedonia: agreement on and demarcation of its border with Kosovo, which threatened to become a source of contention. The Kosovars were initially reluctant to demarcate a border that had been agreed upon not with Pristina but rather with Belgrade, before Kosovo's independence. With assistance from the Organization for Security and Cooperation in Europe, the job nevertheless got done.[20] This vastly improved Skopje's relationship with Pristina. You can look long and hard for two countries that have good relations if the common border is under dispute (witness Pakistan/Afghanistan, for example, not to mention Israel/Palestine, China and its South and East China Sea neighbors). With the border issue on its way to being settled, Macedonia became a friendly neighbor, one that moved quickly to recognize Kosovo as a sovereign state when it declared independence.

The steps backward in Macedonia have often been more apparent than the less dramatic, but important, steps forward. In May 2015 a group of armed Albanians (some in battle dress uniforms) were killed near the Kosovo border by the Macedonian police, who also suffered significant losses. The origins and objectives of the alleged insurgents, at least some of whom appeared to have come from Kosovo, are still not clear. Many Albanians in Macedonia condemned the incursion. Some believe the incident may have been staged by the Macedonian government, or that it turned a blind eye and then intervened against the Albanians for political reasons.[21] Whatever the truth of these allegations, the echo of the 2001 insurgency was all too perceptible. The "Albanian question" is not asked as loudly as the Serbian one, but it lurks in the background in Macedonia and Kosovo.

This incident occurred in the midst of a massive wiretapping scandal in Macedonia, the protagonists of which were rival Macedonian political leaders. Opposition leader Zoran Zaev had for months been releasing tapes and publishing transcripts of telephone conversations among officials of Prime Minister Gruevski's government, some involving the prime minister himself.[22] The content and language were more than disturbing. In one conversation, the then head of the Security and Counter Intelligence Service, a cousin of the prime minister, laughingly talked about having a political opponent raped in prison. Another tape suggested that Gruevski, his interior minister, and other top officials plotted to cover up official responsibility for the death of a twenty-two-year-old beaten by police during Gruevski's 2011 post-election celebrations.[23] The tapes pointed to official involvement in massive violations of human rights, voter fraud, extortion, corruption, fraud, interference in judicial matters, abuse of power, and cover-ups of other malfeasance. Gruevski alleged that the opposition collaborated with a foreign security service to get the taping done, but an EU group of experts determined that Macedonia's own security service did the illegal taping.[24]

The popular reaction was strong, but the electoral consequences were ambiguous. Massive demonstrations that included both Albanians and Macedonians advocated Gruevski's resignation, which occurred in January 2016 in accordance with an EU-brokered and U.S.-supported Przino Agreement providing also for early elections, once the voter rolls were repaired and verified.[25] The elections took place in December 2016, with ambiguous results. Gruevski's party won the most seats in parliament, by two, but both it and its Albanian coalition partner lost seats relative to the previous election. Events and an international push dictated the outcome. Gruevski's supporters were implicated in a bloody attack on a newly elected Albanian Speaker in the parliament chamber in April 2017. That was the last straw for Washington and Brussels. A big diplomatic push from the Europeans and Americans, disgusted with Gruevski's behavior, brought Zaev to power the next month, with support from the Albanian party that had governed with Gruevski.

The Przino Agreement also created a new Special Public Prosecutor. She and her team of prosecutors have exclusive authority to open cases about the crimes exposed in the wiretapping scandal. She faces enormous obstacles, including institutional stonewalling and witness intimidation. A protected witness was found dead in his apartment, shot in the chest. President Ivanov halted investigations of fifty-six officials and their close associates, granting them preemptive pardons in April 2016. Under both domestic and international pressure, he rescinded the amnesties a month later. By mid-2017 the Special Prosecutor had indicted more than ninety people, including former Prime Minister Gruevski. He has been convicted, but so far on relatively minor charges. He faces more serious ones. Anything less than successful high-level prosecutions would contribute to an already entrenched culture of impunity in Macedonia and cast doubt on the potential of the EU and the United States to get Macedonia to deal effectively with corruption and democratic deterioration. Failure of the Special Prosecutor would no doubt also lead to disruptive and violent protests with a highly uncertain and potentially destabilizing outcome.

Once in power, Zaev still faced the name issue. Negotiations were stalled, as Gruevski saw no way of getting a better deal than the status quo: everyone except the Greeks was calling the country "Macedonia" or "Republic of Macedonia." The FYROM was already a member of Partnership for Peace, the NATO anteroom, and had met NATO's *military* criteria for membership. It was at one time the fourth-highest troop contributor per capita to NATO's forces in Afghanistan. Its army fought under U.S. command there and protected NATO headquarters in Kabul.

The Vermont National Guard integrated Macedonian troops with their own fighting force in Afghanistan. The American commander said he relied on them as he would on American troops.[26] Gruevski was getting many of the benefits of NATO membership without having to meet its *political* criteria, which include stable democratic governance, good relations with neighbors, and commitment to the rule of law and human rights. He was far less interested in meeting those requirements. He suffered from what has come to be known as the "Sanader effect," named for the prime minister of Croatia who turned his country definitively toward the EU but was arrested and convicted of corruption charges by its newly independent judiciary. Gruevski had no intention of suffering the same fate.

Greece, whose contributions to NATO in Afghanistan and elsewhere were not greater than Macedonia's, had shown no sign of easing its veto on NATO membership, which it had exercised informally since 2008. Athens had little incentive to do otherwise, as the veto gave it leverage on the name issue. But the impasse aggravated ethnic tension between Macedonia's strongly pro-NATO Albanians and its majority-Macedonian population, which values the country's name more and harbors nationalist passions. It proved impossible to convince the Americans or the Europeans to pressure cash-strapped Greece to resolve the name issue, or at least to allow "The FYROM" the NATO membership it was permitted under the Interim Accord, despite a 15-1 International Court of Justice (ICJ) decision in 2011 favoring that solution.[27] The court also denied Greece's counterclaim that Macedonia had itself violated anti-incitement provisions of the agreement. While Greeks claim that the court failed to adopt any remedies, the decision was a binding one that the ICJ, which relies on sovereign states to implement its decisions, expected Athens to implement without further ado. Greece's failure to do so cast a shadow on its reputation, but without any detectable impact on its position in the dispute.

While the ICJ decision held that the Macedonian government had not legally violated the Interim Accord, it still had its share of moral responsibility. Elected as an economic reformer but blocked from negotiations on EU accession, Gruevski had played to his ethnic nationalist constituency by emphasizing connections to ancient Macedonia that were even more far-fetched than those of his principal adversary, former Greek Prime Minister Samaras. Like the ethnic nationalists in Bosnia, Gruevski and Samaras each gained from antagonism toward the other.

The arguably corrupt and inordinately expensive reconstruction of central Skopje (2010–14) that Gruevski engineered to echo imagined ancient Macedonian greatness is no more than kitsch to most of us, but that does not make it less offensive to someone like Samaras. Those of us who live in Washington, DC, find it hard to complain about faux statues of the ancients, as our capital city was explicitly designed as the "New Rome" and sports many American heroes draped in togas, not to mention a main reading room at the Library of Congress that would make Augustus Caesar blush. No one in Italy has objected—the Italian government has even contributed a few faux Romans to Washington's menagerie. But in the Balkans, ethnic identity is a more sensitive issue. Gruevski's pretensions unquestionably escalated the name dispute.

Samaras fell from power in 2015 and Gruevski in 2017. The leadership changes were decisive. Their less nationalist successors, Alexis Tsipras and Zaev, seized the opportunity to begin serious efforts to resolve the name issue, relying on their capable foreign ministers, Nikos Kotzias and Nikola Dimitrov. Skopje took some unilateral confidence-building steps: it renamed its airport "Skopje International" and a main highway "Friendship," both of which Gruevski had called "Alexander the Great." Athens and Skopje also agreed to an elaborate set of confidence-building measures intended to improve "connectivity" and trust between the two countries in fields such as education, health, culture, justice, and energy. By mid-2018 the two countries had reached agreement, signed at Lake Prespa on their common border, on "Republic of North Macedonia" as the official name (*erga omnes*), though private citizens will continue to call themselves and their language Macedonian.[28] Skopje also acknowledges that Macedonian is a Slavic language without connection to ancient Greece and accepts that it will not interfere in Greece in favor of the ethnic Macedonian minority there. Textbooks and other educational materials are to be reviewed and changed as needed. Both countries forswear any irredentist claims on, or subversive acts toward, the other. Unlike the Dayton Accords, the Prespa Agreement aims to remove drivers of conflict.[29]

NATO responded unequivocally with an invitation, issued at the July 2018 NATO Summit in Brussels, for the Republic of North Macedonia to join the Alliance. The EU was more hesitant, as it faces resistance from several members who want to see reforms within the EU before further enlargement. While that disappointed some, the EU nevertheless has pledged to start accession negotiations with North Macedonia by the end of 2019. Macedonia would benefit enormously from ending frictions that for too long both Macedonian and Greek nationalist leaders have found useful for domestic political purposes, even if doing so is dangerous and destabilizing. But the agreement on the new name still faces serious hurdles. A September 2018 advisory referendum in Macedonia approved the agreement but failed to turn out 50% of registered voters. The agreement was nevertheless approved by a two-thirds margin in the Macedonian parliament, which still however needs to adopt constitutional amendments. The Greek parliament will also have to approve the agreement. The Greek parliament will present a more serious hurdle, as Tsipras' government has a thin majority. "North Macedonia" has elicited opposition demonstrations in both capitals. The Greeks object to "Macedonia." The Macedonians object to "North." Moscow will do its best to amplify nationalist resistance on both sides, as Russia seeks to block any new NATO memberships.[30]

Like other Balkan countries, Macedonia behaves like a bicycle. Without forward motion, it tends to fall over. While the counterfactual is subject to debate, Macedonia's struggles over the past few years would likely not have occurred had it already been a NATO member or a candidate for the EU. Skopje escaped the ravages of war in the Milošević era due in part to deployment of UN peacekeepers from Europe and the United States, stepped back from the brink in 2001 with help from the EU and the United States, recovered sufficiently to enjoy the benefits for fifteen relatively prosperous years, and stepped back from the brink again in 2018, when new leadership in both Skopje and Athens reached a negotiated agreement with assistance from the UN and a lot of encouragement from the EU and the United States. Failure to gain NATO membership and to start accession negotiations with the European Union had blunted the forward momentum of the country's economic reforms and left it vulnerable, but it now has a new opportunity to reach its two most important national goals.

Notes

1. The story of Macedonia's first decade after independence and the international support it got is told in Henryk J. Sokalski, *An Ounce of Prevention: Macedonia and the UN Experience in Preventive Diplomacy* (Washington, DC: United States Institute of Peace Press, 2003); Abiodun Williams, *Preventing War: The United Nations and Macedonia* (Lanham, MD: Rowman & Littlefield, 2000).

2. Thomas S. Szayna and Michele Zanini, "The Yugoslav Retrospective Case, Annex: Demographic Characteristics of Yugoslavia in the Late 1980s," in *Identifying Potential Ethnic Conflicts: Application of a Process Model*, ed. Thomas S. Szayna (Santa Monica, CA: RAND, 1997), 130.
3. Matjaž Klemenčič, "The International Community and the FRY/Belligerents, 1989–1997," in *Confronting the Yugoslav Controversies: A Scholars' Initiative*, ed. Charles W. Ingrao and Thomas Allan Emmert (West Lafayette, IN: Purdue University Press, 2009), 169.
4. Amendment I, *Constitution of the Republic of Macedonia*, http://www.wipo.int/edocs/lexdocs/laws/en/mk/mk014en.pdf.
5. "Macedonia Erases 'Irredentist' Claims as Commission Tables Report," EurActiv.com, last modified April 18, 2013, https://www.euractiv.com/section/enlargement/news/macedonia-erases-irredentist-claims-as-commission-tables-report/; Haralambos Kondonis, "Bilateral Relations between Greece and the Former Yugoslav Republic of Macedonia," in *Athens-Skoplje: An Uneasy Symbiosis, 1995–2002*, ed. Evangelos Kofos and Vlasis Vlasidis (Athens: Papazisis, 2003), 57.
6. United Nations Peacemaker, "Interim Accord between Greece and the Former Yugoslav Republic of Macedonia," September 13, 1995, https://peacemaker.un.org/greecefyrom-interimaccord95.
7. John Cam Hobhouse, *A Journey through Albania and Other Provinces of Turkey in Europe and Asia, to Constantinople, during the Years 1809 and 1810* (London: Printed for James Cawthorn, 1813).
8. TV Sonce, "Samaras-English," YouTube Video, 4:43, January 27, 2009, https://www.youtube.com/watch?v=QnCrRXJAJeU.
9. There is little genetic evidence of connection to the ancient Greeks, or variation among any of the Balkans ethnicities, except possibly the Vlachs (aka Aromuns). See E. Bosch et al., "Paternal and Maternal Lineages in the Balkans Show a Homogeneous Landscape over Linguistic Barriers, Except for the Isolated Aromuns," *Annals of Human Genetics* 70, no. 4 (July 2006): 459–87, http://www.carswell.com.au/wp-content/documents/homogenous-balkan-analysis.pdf.
10. Doneo Donev, Silvana Onceva, and Ilija Gligorov, "Refugee Crisis in Macedonia during the Kosovo Conflict in 1999," *Croatian Medical Journal* 43, no. 2 (2002): 184–89, http://neuron.mefst.hr/docs/CMJ/issues/2002/43/2/11885045.pdf.
11. Veton Surroi, *The Book of Butterflies* (Pristina: Koha, 2013). Surroi tells the story of the political negotiations in which he played an important role, but he repeatedly claims he did not know who constituted the National Liberation Army. Ali Ahmeti, its leader and now a leading politician in Macedonia, told me in April 2018 that the rebellion was plotted from Switzerland, with capabilities built up as early as the 1990s.

12. Nevena Dimova, "Macedonian and Albanian Intellectuals and the National Idea(s) in Socialist Macedonia," in *Avatars of Intellectuals under Communism*, ed. Corina Palasan and Cristian Vasile, *History of Communism in Europe* 2 (2011): 244–45.
13. Peace Accords Matrix, "Ohrid Agreement," Kroc Institute for International Peace Studies University of Notre Dame, August 13, 2001, https://peaceaccords.nd.edu/accord/ohrid-agreement.
14. European Stability Initiative, "The Ohrid Agreement and Its Implementation," https://www.esiweb.org/index.php?lang=en&id=563.
15. Demush Bajrami and Arburim Iseni, "The Challenge of (Non) Implementation of the Ohrid Framework Agreement in the Republic of Macedonia," *European Scientific Journal* 10, no. 10 (April 2014): 203–18.
16. "Cablegate: Macedonia: The Ohrid Framework Agreement," Scoop Wikileaks, January 6, 2010, https://balkanleaks.eu/242.
17. EUR-Lex, "The Principle of Subsidiarity, Glossary of Summaries," https://eur-lex.europa.eu/summary/glossary/subsidiarity.html.
18. Florian Bieber et al., *Power Sharing and the Implementation of the Ohrid Framework Agreement* (Skopje: Friedrich Ebert Shtiftung, Office Macedonia, 2008), http://library.fes.de/pdf-files/bueros/skopje/06357.pdf.
19. 2018 Index of Economic Freedom the Heritage Foundation, "Macedonia" (2018), https://www.heritage.org/international-economies/commentary/2018-index-economic-freedom.
20. Unrepresented Nations and Peoples Organization, "Kosova: Border Demarcation Begins," August 24, 2012, http://www.unpo.org/article/14753.
21. Benjamin Arifi, "Smoke and Mirrors: A Macedonian Spy Mystery," *Balkan Insight*, May 9, 2018, http://www.balkaninsight.com/en/article/smoke-and-mirrors-a-macedonian-spy-mystery-05-08-2018.
22. Radio Free Europe/Radio Liberty, "The Explainer: Roots of Macedonia's Political Crisis Run Deep," https://www.rferl.org/a/explainer-crisis-in-macedonia-leads-to-violent-protests/27675969.html.
23. "Macedonia Officials Attempted Murder Coverup," *Balkan Insight*, May 15, 2015, http://www.balkaninsight.com/en/article/macedonia-officials-attempted-murder-cover-up-opposition-claims.
24. *The Former Yugoslav Republic of Macedonia: Recommendations of the Senior Experts' Group on Systemic Rule of Law Issues Relating to the Communications Interception Revealed in Spring 2015*, Brussels June 8, 2015, https://ec.europa.eu/neighbourhood-enlargement/sites/near/files/news_corner/news/news-files/20150619_recommendations_of_the_senior_experts_group.pdf.

25. The Przino Agreement is at https://ec.europa.eu/neighbourhood-enlargement/sites/near/files/news_corner/news/news-files/20150619_agreement.pdf and "Statement by Commissioner Hahn and MEPs Vajgl, Howitt and Kukan: Agreement in Skopje to Overcome Political Crisis," European Union, July 2015, http://europa.eu/rapid/press-release_STATEMENT-15-5372_en.htm.
26. Daniel Serwer, "The Western Balkans and the 2012 NATO Summit," Hearing before the Commission on Security and Cooperation in Europe: US Helsinki Commission, January 18, 2012, https://evergreen.lib.in.us/eg/opac/record/19788997.
27. International Court of Justice, "Application of the Interim Accord of 13 September 1995 (the Former Yugoslav Republic of Macedonia v. Greece)," http://www.icj-cij.org/en/case/142.
28. Final Agreement for the Settlement of the Differences as Described in the United Nations Security Council Resolutions 817 (1993) and 845 (1993), the Termination of the Interim Accord of 1995, and the Establishment of a Strategic Partnership between the Parties, http://www.pappaspost.com/wp-content/uploads/2018/06/Athens-Skopje-English.pdf.
29. Edward P. Joseph and Ognen Vangelov, "Breakthrough in the Balkans: Macedonia's New Name," *Survival* 60, no. 4 (2018): 37–44, https://doi.org/10.1080/00396338.2018.1495426.
30. Saska Cvetkovska, "Russian Businessman behind Unrest in Macedonia," Organized Crime and Corruption Reporting Project, July 16, 2018, https://www.occrp.org/en/28-ccwatch/cc-watch-indepth/8329-russian-businessman-behind-unrest-in-macedonia.

Open Access This chapter is distributed under the terms of the Creative Commons Attribution 4.0 International License (http://creativecommons.org/licenses/by/4.0/), which permits use, duplication, adaptation, distribution and reproduction in any medium or format, as long as you give appropriate credit to the original author(s) and the source, a link is provided to the Creative Commons license and any changes made are indicated.

The images or other third party material in this chapter are included in the work's Creative Commons license, unless indicated otherwise in the credit line; if such material is not included in the work's Creative Commons license and the respective action is not permitted by statutory regulation, users will need to obtain permission from the license holder to duplicate, adapt or reproduce the material.

CHAPTER 5

Kosovo and Serbia: Loveless Marriage, Difficult Divorce

Abstract In Kosovo and Serbia, the ingredients of war were all salient: Yugoslavia's breakup, Milošević's political ambitions as well as military capabilities, and ethnic nationalism. A last-ditch diplomatic push failed to prevent war, precipitating NATO's second Balkan intervention and deployment. Now independent Kosovo is a product of luxury state-building, including NATO-led troops, UN administration, and a massive EU rule-of-law mission. But Kosovo's sovereignty and democratic transition are still incomplete. Serbia's postwar course was less internationalized, more organic, and more equivocal. Serbia lost control of Kosovo south of the Ibar River. Elections and popular protests removed Milošević but failed to hold Serbian nationalism accountable. Belgrade aims for EU membership, but autocratic inclinations and strong ties with Russia threaten to divert it.

Keywords Security Council Resolution 1244 · Standards before/with status · Ahtisaari Plan · April 2013 Brussels Agreement

As we have seen, Bosnia had the three ingredients of Balkan war in spades. The result was more than one war. In Macedonia, Milošević's political ambitions and Serbian nationalism were negligible factors. The result was a delayed and relatively small conflict. It was Albanians, not Serbs, who eventually brought war to Macedonia. In Kosovo, the three ingredients again formed an explosive mixture.

Kosovar aspirations before the breakup of former Yugoslavia had been limited.[1] Communist Kosovars wanted to gain full status as a republic in former Yugoslavia, rather than continuing as an autonomous province nominally inside Serbia, albeit one with its own parliament, police force, courts, and a representative on the rotating collective presidency, like the six Yugoslav republics. But with the dissolution of Yugoslavia, Kosovars no longer felt constrained to remain in a federation that Serbia would dominate once Slovenia and Croatia had left. Their ambitions shifted to independence.

Milošević's political ambitions were a key factor.[2] He discovered in 1987, when he spoke in Kosovo at a Serb protest against alleged Albanian mistreatment, the power of Serbian nationalism to mobilize political support. "No one should dare to beat you," he declared, beginning his own transformation into a Serbian nationalist. He showed no concern for the beatings Serbs delivered to Albanians. Ethnic nationalism in a multiethnic context requires exclusionary politics. Milošević rode the wave of Serbian nationalism and its anti-Albanian impetus to the presidency of the Serbian League of Communists. He also engineered constitutional amendments ending Kosovo's autonomy, which were approved in the Kosovo assembly under Serbian pressure, but without the two-thirds majority required, in March 1989.

Milošević's infamous appearance at the six hundredth anniversary of the battle of Kosovo Polje on Vidovdan (St. Vitus Day, June 28) that year was the culmination of his conversion from Yugoslav Communist apparatchik to Serbian nationalist demagogue, though Serbs and Albanians (who were not yet predominantly Muslim) fought on both sides. Kosovo Albanians today are no less inclined to view the battle of Kosovo Polje through ethnic nationalist lenses than are Serbs.

With Kosovo deprived of its autonomy, the Albanian members of the Kosovo assembly met in the summer of 1990 to declare Kosovo a republic, albeit still within Yugoslavia. Serbia responded by dissolving the assembly and the Kosovo government as well as sometime later dismissing 80,000 Albanians from their government jobs. Milošević was ending more than twenty years of Albanian participation in Kosovo's governance under Yugoslav rule by excluding them from the state. Only Serbs, who likely represented no more than 10% of the population, would henceforth govern Kosovo. "Kosovo is Serbia" became the battle cry.

Ethnic repression fed ethnic rebellion. As Milošević expelled the Albanians from Kosovo's institutions, Albanian literary scholar Ibrahim Rugova led a mainly nonviolent Albanian rebellion, without, however, any real sense of how it could achieve the goal of independence.[3] Inspired by the independence of Slovenia and Croatia, a "parallel" assembly declared Kosovo a sovereign and independent republic in 1991 and held elections in 1992. The Kosovars also created separate parastatal institutions, including an education system that met in homes and basements, a health system administered by the Mother Teresa Society, and a government funded with contributions mainly from the diaspora and run by ordinary people who contributed labor, real estate, and expertise.[4]

In the 1990s only Albania recognized Kosovo's sovereignty, which remained a dead letter. The Yugoslav police and army were still very much in charge, even if the parallel state provided education and health services to the Albanian population. The international community was not ready for an independent Kosovo. It was preoccupied with the Bosnian War and with protecting Macedonia. Kosovo got short shrift. There were unofficial attempts to mediate the conflict between Belgrade and Pristina, especially an effort by the Italian Catholic charity Sant'Egidio to reopen the public schools to Albanians. That and other initiatives to manage or resolve the conflict came to naught.

The failure of the Kosovars to get a hearing at the Dayton talks in late 1995 pushed them in a direction some were already headed: toward violent insurrection. They took up arms, many obtained from Albania. State authority there evaporated in 1996, after the collapse of Ponzi schemes in which a large portion of the population lost hard-earned money. Weapons circulated widely. It is not surprising that many found their way over the mountains into Kosovo to a small guerrilla force that dubbed itself the Kosovo Liberation Army (KLA).

As with many other guerrilla insurgencies, the KLA's role was not entirely military in its objectives. While it focused mainly on killing Serbian police, it could not defeat them or the JNA, but it could attract international attention by precipitating Serbian crackdowns and atrocities. Milošević obliged, driving even more Kosovars to arms and largely vaporizing the nonviolent street demonstrations Rugova promoted. Photo coverage of a massacre in Drenica in February 1998 aroused condemnation in international public opinion.[5]

Serbs value Kosovo, sometimes called the "Serb Jerusalem," far more than Bosnia. The first Serbian kingdom was founded there. Kosovo still hosts many important Serb monasteries, cemeteries, and other religious sites. This made it more important to Milošević's image as a defender of Serbs than Bosnia, where he had competition for Serb leadership from Republika Srpska President Karadžić. In Kosovo, he was *the* man. Serb paramilitary leaders "Arkan" (Željko Ražnatović) and Vojislav Šešelj, responsible for a good deal of havoc in Kosovo, were more agents than competitors. Milošević sought to subjugate the province. He cleansed the border area with Albania of Albanians and continued a draconian crackdown against the KLA, which was largely successful militarily. Between 100,000 and 200,000 people were chased from their homes during the final months of 1998. Milošević also tried to impose the Serbian language, make Albanians uncomfortable with remaining in Kosovo, and import Serb settlers from among the refugees who had left Croatia in 1995.

Milošević's efforts precipitated international civilian intervention, first with the deployment of the Kosovo Diplomatic Observer Mission and then the still civilian Kosovo Verification Mission (KVM) of the Organization for Security and Co-operation in Europe (OSCE). These worthy diplomatic efforts were too little, too late.[6] In January 1999 the Račak massacre of forty-five civilians attracted wide international attention, when American diplomat and KVM leader Bill Walker labeled it a crime against humanity, perpetrated, he said, by Serbian security forces.[7] That consolidated international willingness to stop not only what Milošević was already doing to the Kosovo Albanians but also his anticipated plans for expelling Albanians from Kosovo en masse, which were known to Western intelligence.[8]

The French-hosted talks at Rambouillet in early 1999 were a last-ditch effort to prevent that from happening and avoid military intervention. They failed because the effort was poorly conceived. Many in the State Department believed the NATO bombing had forced Milošević to end the war in Bosnia. They repeated ad infinitum that he would only respond to the credible threat of force. That was a misconception of what made him yield at Dayton. Milošević was not concerned with the threat of force per se. He came to Dayton suing for peace not because force was used but because he feared the NATO bombing would precipitate an exodus of Serbs from Bosnia that would endanger his hold on power in Serbia. Serbian nationalist sentiment was far stronger about Kosovo than about the Serb-inhabited portions of Croatia or Bosnia. If Milošević failed to keep Kosovo, he anticipated a serious threat to his hold on power. By the same token, he would consolidate his position with ethnic nationalists if he could rid Kosovo of a good part of its Albanian population.

The Serbian forces came close to achieving this objective, with the expulsion from their homes of 600,000–700,000 Albanians after NATO started bombing in March 1999. There was far less killing than in Bosnia (about 10,000 Albanians were killed), and no concentration camps, which had attracted unwanted international attention in Bosnia. The Serbian security forces had learned how to get large numbers of people to move without rounding them up or killing them. The main mode of operation was to kill a prominent citizen in the main square, leave his body there, and then order everyone else to leave. This technique moved a lot of people, without much need for logistics to support the operation. Many Kosovars hopped on whatever means of transportation they could find and left.

In the end, NATO bombing succeeded when Milošević found himself unexpectedly indicted by the International Criminal Tribunal for the former Yugoslavia, concerned about fading Russian support, and advised that damage done to Serbia's infrastructure could be irreversible and make recovery impossible. That would really threaten Milošević's hold on power. He yielded.[9] But neither he nor his successors acknowledged responsibility for the atrocities that had been committed, the "historical truth" that is required for accountability.[10]

Here the narrative splits. Serbia in June 1999 went one way. Kosovo went another.

Serbia's state and civil society emerged from the war intact, except for the amputation of most of Kosovo. Serbia retreated but did not surrender. Milošević remained in power, with his security forces barely scathed. Kosovo north of the Ibar River, which contained three municipalities with prewar Serb majorities, remained under Belgrade's surreptitious control, in addition to the northern half of Mitrovica/Mitrovicë. French NATO troops protected the mostly Serb population in these three and a half northern municipalities. Except for a relatively few individuals, Serbian civil society had opposed the NATO bombing, even if many of its supporters opposed Milošević. This made international support for Serbian nongovernmental organizations fade during and immediately after the war, but it preserved the credibility of Serbia's extensive network of civil society organizations with at least a portion of the general population. They would soon need it.

Belgrade had already faced a nonviolent rebellion against Milošević's rule in the winter of 1996–1997. The opposition group Zajedno

(Together) protested against Milošević's falsification of municipal election results. The demonstrations fizzled once Milošević gave into a part of the street's demands and the Americans renewed contacts with him, which had been suspended. But by the spring of 1998 it was clear to many that U.S. policy, which had relied on Milošević at Dayton and would do so again at Rambouillet, was ill-conceived. He was part of the problem and not part of the solution, especially for Kosovo.[11]

This implied getting rid of him. A small group, including people with intimate knowledge of the Polish Solidarity movement that had brought down Communism in Warsaw as well as others involved in the collapse of Communism in Eastern Europe, convened at the U.S. Institute of Peace. They offered two suggestions: first, it was unlikely anything could be done, as Milošević had been elected in more or less free if not fair elections; and second, the best bet would be to support a broad spectrum of democratically minded organizations, a "coalition of coalitions," rather than any particular political grouping or leader. This made a good deal of sense, as civil society in Serbia was robust, partly due to support from George Soros, while the opposition political parties and their leaders were neither unified nor capable. They were also more inclined toward Serbian nationalism, which they found necessary to compete politically, and readier to cooperate with Milošević.

Testifying in December 1998 at the Helsinki Commission of the U.S. Congress, I put forward a proposal for an additional $50 million of assistance to Serbian civil society over two years.[12] By January, two things had happened. First, three deputy prime ministers of Serbia appeared on the primetime newscast in Belgrade waving a document they claimed was a top-secret CIA plot to overthrow Milošević. It was my public testimony, downloaded from the Internet, provided an official-looking seal, and stamped "top secret," as I confirmed to a courageous reporter at the Belgrade daily *Blic* the next day. The second thing was more important but less visible: Helsinki Commission chair Congressman Chris Smith began to prepare legislation proposing the kind of program I had suggested. The State Department asked USAID to preempt the effort. Money started flowing to the student movement Otpor! (Resistance!), the voting-rights organization CeSID (Center for Free Elections and Democracy), and other Serbian civil society organizations committed to democracy.

By the summer of 1999 the war was over. Milošević looked shaky, even though assistance to his democratic opponents, suspended during the war, had not yet resumed. War damage was much in evidence. There were spontaneous anti-Milošević demonstrations, even in the central province of Šumadija, which had been a stronghold of Serbian nationalism. By failing to turn on the taps of assistance to Serbian civil society, the West likely missed an early opportunity to unseat Milošević.

A year later he was feeling confident again and decided to call early elections for the presidency and parliament of Yugoslavia, which then consisted only of Serbia and Montenegro. That was a big mistake, as was allowing domestic observers and posting results at the polling places. Otpor! pressed the opposition politicians to unify (which, except for firebrand Vuk Draskovic, they did) and helped get out the vote, along with the trade unions and other civil society organizations. CeSID knew the results before the Milošević regime could falsify them. They also blocked him from stuffing the Kosovo ballot boxes. The opposition chose nationalist Vojislav Koštunica to run against Milošević, because American polling showed he had broader appeal and fewer "negatives" than the more liberal, less nationalist, and more prominent opposition leader Zoran Đinđić. Koštunica sneaked over the 50% threshold by a narrow margin, one significantly smaller than the number of non-Serb, minority voters who opted for him. The opposition also won a majority in parliament.

People often remember Milošević as falling to street demonstrators led by Otpor! and chanting "Gotov je!" (He's finished!). They were demonstrations in favor of recognizing known election results. This was not revolution. It was a successful nonviolent campaign in favor of known election results. Serbian institutions remained in place. By December, the opposition had also won Serbian parliamentary and presidential elections, which made Đinđić prime minister of Serbia.

Milošević really was finished. Đinđić had him arrested in March 2001 and transferred to The Hague on June 28, Vidovdan. There he faced multiple charges of war crimes and crimes against humanity brought by the prosecutor of the International Criminal Tribunal for the former Yugoslavia, created in the early 1990s when Washington was unwilling to contemplate military intervention but wanted some visible response to the horrors of the Bosnian War. He was on trial there for crimes committed in Bosnia and Croatia as well as Kosovo when he died in 2006, of causes later determined to have been natural.[13]

Đinđić was assassinated in March 2003 by people associated with both Milošević's security forces and organized crime gangs, which by then were virtually indistinguishable. The smuggling required to get around sanctions made them natural allies. People have been tried and convicted for the murder of Đinđić, but who gave the orders or tacitly approved has not been clarified.[14] Boris Tadić was elected to succeed Đinđić as president of Serbia in 2004. Tadić apologized to both Bosnia and Croatia for crimes committed in the name of the Serbian people, but not to Kosovo, whose territory he, Koštunica, and later Serbian President Tomislav Nikolić continued to claim as an integral part of Serbia.

Tadić presided over the formal dissolution of what had become the State Union of Serbia and Montenegro, following a 2006 referendum in Montenegro that made it over an EU-required 55% threshold by a hair. Again the margin was smaller than the number of ethnic minority citizens (mainly Albanians and Bosniaks), who voted for Montenegro's independence. Inclusion, like exclusion, has political consequences.

Deprived of Montenegro, Serbia replaced its Communist-era constitution in late 2006 with one that defines "Kosovo and Metohija" ("Metohija" refers to "church lands," which before Communism were extensive in Kosovo) as an integral part of Serbia with ill-defined substantial autonomy.[15] Kosovo Albanians, who had been boycotting Serbian elections for many years, were not counted on the voter rolls in the referendum that approved the new constitution. Had they been, the referendum could not have met the legal requirement that 50% of those registered needed to vote. No one, however, challenged the referendum on the obvious grounds that Albanians had been denied their right to block the referendum by not voting. The international community welcomed the new constitution, the referendum for which had essentially treated the Kosovo Albanians as non-citizens.

If the Kosovo Albanians were not counted as citizens of Serbia, they had to be citizens of something else. It is hard to imagine what that might be other than an independent Kosovo.

Serbia even without Milošević did nothing to make it attractive for Kosovo Albanians to remain inside the Serbian state. A timid politician who feared being outflanked in the nationalist direction, Tadić accomplished little in his second term (2008–2012). The election of the far more nationalist opposition leader Tomislav Nikolić to the presidency of Serbia in 2012 was the first real alternation in power since the fall of Milošević. Nikolić delegated handling of both the EU and Kosovo to his political partner, Aleksandar Vučić, deputy prime minister from 2012 to 2014, subsequently prime minister, and now president. Vučić had also been a Milošević loyalist but decided to throw in his lot with the West, at least insofar as EU membership was concerned. While President Nikolić was busy giving medals to Belarusan strongman Lukashenko, Vučić was busy getting Serbia candidacy for the EU and resolving lots of issues with Kosovo, apart from its political status. He won early parliamentary elections in April 2016 and then the presidency in April 2017. Serbia still faces serious issues in its own democratization: corruption, government control over the media, and a less than fully independent court system that takes its own good time in resolving cases. There has been little progress during the last few years in prosecuting the war crimes of the 1990s.[16] But the big question is: How will Serbia handle Kosovo?

Before answering that question, we need to turn back to 2001 to catch up with what had been going on in Pristina.[17] The NATO/Yugoslavia war ended not with a peace treaty but rather with a "military-technical agreement," which provided for JNA withdrawal from Kosovo, and UN Security Council Resolution 1244, which acknowledged Yugoslav sovereignty in the nonbinding preamble but also foresaw a political resolution of Kosovo's status consistent with the will of its people, which had been obvious and irreversible for more than a decade.[18] Resolution 1244 essentially imposed an interim United Nations administration (UNMIK) and made the question of the legality of the NATO/Yugoslavia war irrelevant, while postponing a "final status" decision to a process not clearly defined. Welcome again to the world of international compromises. As in Bosnia, Milošević was good at snatching ambiguity from the jaws of certain defeat. The international community was looking for an elite political process. No grassroots reconciliation effort was contemplated, and little occurred. But some mistakes from the Bosnia experience were avoided. From the first, the UN Special Representative of the Secretary-General was given powers to hire and fire as well as impose legislation, which amounted to the equivalent of the "Bonn powers." He was also given a coordinating role with other intergovernmental organizations working in Kosovo. He and the NATO-led Kosovo Force (KFOR) military commander were instructed to cooperate closely.

While NATO was preoccupied with the negotiations that ended the NATO/Yugoslavia war, Russia moved a contingent of its troops from Bosnia, where they had served for years under American command, to the Pristina airport. This quick maneuver was intended to be prelude to the arrival of more Russian troops by air, to seize and "protect" Serb areas of Kosovo, especially the three and a half municipalities north of the Ibar River. NATO members and aspirants refused overflight clearances for the Russian aircraft, prevented them from arriving in Pristina, and eventually offered the Russians a face-saving role in KFOR. Russian President Yeltsin yielded, but his maneuver foreshadowed future Russian resistance under Vladimir Putin to NATO's role in the Balkans.

The Kosovo Albanians returned home fast, en masse, defying UN expectations of a slower, planned, and orderly return. Farmers wanted to get back to their homes and plant their crops. Urbanites feared waiting would allow squatters. Once the JNA and Serbian police forces were withdrawn under the watchful eye of KFOR, Albanians felt safe and went home as quickly as they could to the 85% or so of the territory south of the Ibar River. There the French peacekeepers drew the line the Russians had intended to draw, fearing that Albanian returns north of the Ibar would lead to expulsion of Serbs from northern Kosovo.

The KLA, feeling triumphant, appointed mayors to replace those named by "President" Rugova before the war. Violence between Albanians increased sharply, as frictions between the KLA and Rugova's party, the Democratic League of Kosovo (LDK), heightened. The Serbian state that had governed Kosovo before the war was gone. The Albanian civil society organizations that had done so much to provide education and health after the expulsion of Albanians from the Serbian administration were struggling. International nongovernmental organizations and the newly installed UN administration of the province were hiring away all their English-speakers and beginning to compete in service provision.

All politics is local, but too often in postwar situations the impulse to skimp on local politics and hold national elections as quickly as possible is irresistible. In Bosnia the Americans had compelled the OSCE to hold national elections within a year after the Dayton agreements, to satisfy a presidential desire for demonstrable progress. The polls predictably installed ethnic nationalists. In Kosovo, the UN avoided that mistake. Municipal elections that swept away many of the KLA-appointed mayors in favor of LDK competitors were held in October 2000, underlining that politics, including local service delivery, rather than force would be dominant in the postwar period. Hashim Thaçi, then a KLA political leader often regarded as an American favorite, would remain important but not rise to power in Pristina until years later.

In the meanwhile, the UN successfully stood up first the Kosovo Administrative Council and later the Provisional Institutions of Self-Government. The first Kosovo-wide elections (not, however, held in the Serb-controlled north) chose a legislative assembly in 2001. The newly installed assembly elected Rugova president in 2002. While still under UN administration, Kosovo was already beginning to grow democratic institutions but remained without a fully developed administrative apparatus. Recognizing the anomaly, the UN administrators were anxious to devolve responsibility to Kosovans, as the citizens (Serb, Albanian, and others) of the province are properly denominated.

The basic idea was "standards before status": Kosovo would need to earn a decision on political status by ensuring the international community that it could govern a multiethnic and democratic society in accordance with international human rights standards.[19] International tutelage was intense. The police force began to be known for its good training and professionalism, instilled by the OSCE, although the courts remained unimpressive.[20] In addition to police training, the OSCE played a significant role in building democratic institutions, especially the parliament and the electoral process. Many other intergovernmental and nongovernmental international organizations were also involved, including WHO, UNESCO, the International Organization for Migration, and the UN High Commissioner for Refugees.[21] The World Health Organization, for example, drove the reestablishment of the health care system, which proved difficult because of lack of capacity to implement its well-designed scheme.[22] UNESCO played a similar role in the reestablishment of the education system.[23]

Positive momentum came to an abrupt halt with ethnic riots in March 2004. The rioting was the result of a series of inventions, misunderstandings, exaggerations, and overreactions of a sort that had happened repeatedly in Kosovo before the war.[24] The Albanian-language radio and TV contributed substantially to inciting the violence.[25] The consequences were serious. Eight Serbs and eleven Albanians were killed. The damage to Serb churches and communities was substantial. Thousands of Serbs were forced from their homes. The international community feared that worse might be in the offing. The UN secretary-general commissioned Norwegian diplomat Kai Eide to have a hard look at the situation.

Eide concluded that the political status quo was unsustainable.[26] Albanian aspirations were frustrated. Reintegration with Serbia, which had done nothing to make it attractive, was impossible. The UN therefore embarked on the final status negotiations foreseen in Resolution 1244, presided over by UN Special Envoy Martti Ahtisaari, a former president of Finland, with support from professional diplomats Frank Wisner for the United States and Wolfgang Ischinger for the EU.[27] Their effort resulted in a plan intended to make Kosovo independence palatable to Belgrade.[28] It essentially incorporated everything Belgrade asked for. Ahtisaari's recommendation to the UN secretary-general that Kosovo should become independent was separate from the plan, but part of his overall approach.[29]

Serbia declined to sign on despite the extensive provisions for protection of Serbs. The Americans and Europeans nevertheless insisted that the Kosovo government adopt and implement the Ahtisaari Plan, as a condition for support of independence, and accept a huge EU rule-of-law mission (EULEX) to nurture the judicial sector. Once again, as in Bosnia, the Americans and Europeans found it easier to twist the arm of their friends rather their adversaries in Belgrade. The plan included the idea that Kosovo would not—and would not be permitted—to unify with any neighboring state or part of any neighboring state. This constitutional provision was intended to protect Macedonia as well as Serbia, both of which have Albanian-majority areas that border Kosovo. It was also intended to prevent the formation of Greater Albania. The answer to the Albanian question was no: Albanians will not live in one state but in several.

Essentially what we have here is a deal, in the absence of one between Serbia and Kosovo, between the West, including the United States and most of the EU, and the Kosovo Albanians: Kosovo got independence, but that ruled out Greater Kosovo (Kosovo plus the Albanian portions of Macedonia) and Greater Albania. Pristina was obliged to provide what Belgrade failed to provide to Albanians: a high degree of protection and positive discrimination to Serbs. Status would come with standards. Not everyone in Kosovo accepts this deal. The Vetëvendosje (Self-determination) movement dislikes it and still wants a referendum on union with Albania. It attracted less than 15% of the vote in the 2014 parliamentary election but in 2017 rose to 27.5% to become the second largest bloc in parliament before splitting in 2018. The Serb contingent in the Kosovo parliament also rejects the constitution and regards Kosovo as still an autonomous province of Serbia.

Serbia often describes Kosovo's independence declaration in February 2008 as unilateral, which it was from Serbia's perspective. Belgrade disapproved. It lined up, and still maintains, support from Moscow in the UN Security Council that blocks Kosovo membership in the UN General Assembly and in other international organizations. But Kosovo independence was well coordinated with those European countries amenable to it and with the United States. It is now recognized by more than one hundred sovereign states, not, however, including five members of the EU and four members of NATO. Kosovo substantially completed its obligations to implement the Ahtisaari Plan in 2012, ending supervision by an International Civilian Office (ICO), but a rump UN mission remains in Kosovo under Resolution 1244.[30]

The record of state-building in Kosovo is, however, far from pristine. Pristina benefited before and after independence from three major international missions: UNMIK, EULEX, and the ICO. They have been roundly criticized as ineffectual in improving the country's governance, which has arguably stagnated or even deteriorated since independence according to World Bank statistics.[31] Kosovo's governance remains on most dimensions at the lower end of the regional scale, along with Albania's. This mediocre performance is due at least in part to the continuing preoccupation of Kosovo's politicians and electorate with the country's still incomplete sovereignty, including the contest between those who want Kosovo to remain an independent state and those who prefer union with Albania. So long as sovereignty issues remain open, Kosovo politicians will find they can gain more votes by waving nationalist flags than by delivering jobs and economic growth. The Europeans and Americans have also hesitated to upset the applecart by allowing those who favor union with Albania to come to power, which limits the possibilities for alternation.

The Serbia and Kosovo stories re-converged with German Chancellor Angela Merkel's visit to Belgrade in August 2011. Angered by Serb attacks in northern Kosovo (including on German peacekeepers), she read Serbia the riot act, insisting on reintegration of the northern, Serb-controlled Kosovo municipalities with Kosovo south of the Ibar. Since then, under EU tutelage, Pristina and Belgrade have managed to reach agreement with Belgrade on half a dozen "technical" issues as well as political reintegration of the Serb-dominated north into Kosovo, in accordance with the Ahtisaari Plan, as well as creation of an association of Serb municipalities, not yet implemented.[32]

Belgrade was rewarded for this April 2013 Brussels Agreement with Pristina with its much-coveted candidacy for the EU, which makes available money and technical assistance needed to help prepare for EU accession. Complete normalization of relations with Kosovo is a requirement for Serbian EU accession. Precisely what that means remains unspecified, but in practice there are many EU members that will refuse to approve accession without Serbian recognition of Kosovo's sovereignty and territorial integrity. Pristina received a less rich but still appetizing Stabilization and Association Agreement, as well as the promise of a visa waiver program once it met all the technical requirements. That it did by mid-2018. It remains to be seen whether the politics of an increasingly xenophobic EU will permit implementation, though the merits of Kosovans being able to travel freely in Europe and witness its economics firsthand are compelling. While far from resolving everything, the 2013 Brussels Agreement substantially reduced passions, and uncertainties, on both sides.

Nineteen years ago, Kosovo was a province inside Serbia. Today it is independent in the sense that it governs itself, but it is not entirely sovereign. At each stage of its evolution during these nearly two decades it got less than what Albanian Kosovars wanted, but it never slid backwards. At the end of the war it became a UN protectorate offered status if it met standards. Kai Eide's report proposed ending the protectorate and offered status with standards. The Ahtisaari Plan implemented that idea. Independence came only with supervision and constraints on sovereignty that are gradually loosening. EULEX international judges and prosecutors, for example, ended their "executive" role in 2018.

There are still big issues. Kosovo has failed to meet even minimal goals for the environment, education, and women.[33] The EU still maintains monitoring and police missions in Kosovo, an internationally staffed but nominally "Kosovo" court is operating in The Hague to prosecute war crimes and crimes against humanity that occurred between 1998 and 2000, the UN still maintains a symbolic presence consistent with Resolution 1244, and NATO is still responsible for Kosovo's territorial defense. NATO will want to draw down as Kosovo builds up its own security forces, provided they perform professionally. The current lightly armed security forces will need to be converted into a small army. Belgrade hopes to prevent this, by blocking a constitutional amendment some think required. Albanians believe it can be done through legislation.[34]

Sovereignty issues arouse fierce domestic political tensions. Vetëvendosje in late 2015 and early 2016 led violent protests, including in parliament, against two alleged infractions against Kosovo's sovereignty: demarcation of the border with Montenegro and establishment of the association of Serb municipalities. The border issue has been resolved. The association of Serb municipalities is still an issue, because the Pristina authorities fear it will be used to establish a de facto separate governing structure for the Serbs, like Republika Srpska in Bosnia. Albanian nationalism could still put stability in the Balkans at risk if Kosovo is unable to complete its sovereignty.

The big question mark is whether, or when, Serbia will recognize Kosovo as a sovereign state. Belgrade politicians are fond of saying that Serbia will never recognize Kosovo's "unilateral declaration of independence." But it does not have to, because no one does. A declaration of independence is a political document, not a legal one. What sovereign states recognize is the sovereignty of another state, which entails its control over territory, the legitimacy of its government, and its monopoly on the use of force.[35] Today this is often done not bilaterally, but through admission of a state to the United Nations.

Belgrade has already recognized Kosovo's sovereignty implicitly, as the 2013 Brussels Agreement acknowledges the validity of Pristina's constitution and judicial system on the whole territory of Kosovo, without reference to Serbia. It also contains a provision that acknowledges Serbia and Kosovo will each qualify for and enter the EU separately, without trying to block the other. Since only sovereign states can become EU members, this was an implicit recognition of Kosovo's inevitable sovereignty. It is now generally accepted even in Belgrade that Serbia will in due course have to amend its constitution to accommodate the facts of life, though how it will do so is still unclear.

The harder-nosed negotiators in Belgrade will want to hold out until the last minute, figuring that the EU will be prepared to pay a higher price for Kosovo recognition later rather than sooner. Or, some hope, Serbia will be able to enter the EU first and use its veto to block Kosovo's accession, though the EU's experience with Cyprus will make many members wary of that scenario. The simple fact is that Serbia will not be able to enter the EU without resolving all its issues with Kosovo, because one or more of the twenty-three EU members (twenty-two after Brexit) that have recognized Kosovo will not allow it. Pristina has worked hard to convince the five "non-recognizing" EU members (Spain, Romania, Slovakia, Greece, and Cyprus) to change their minds, but without success. Decisions to recognize by one or two of them would bring a lot of pressure on Belgrade to settle the matter sooner rather than later. A 2010 International Court of Justice advisory opinion that found Kosovo independence breached no international law opens the door to recognition but does not require it.[36]

Even Serbian recognition, however, will not necessarily get Kosovo into the UN. Russia has its own reasons to continue to block the UN

Security Council recommendation required before the General Assembly can vote on UN membership. At the very least, Moscow will seek as a quid pro quo Washington's acceptance of the independence of South Ossetia and Abkhazia, its two "independent" clients in Georgia, as well as acceptance of the annexation of Crimea.

One possible outcome that Moscow would like, because it would legitimize the precedent of changing borders to accommodate ethnic differences, involves an exchange of territory and population between Kosovo and Serbia. The "divide and govern" strategy that has prevailed in Kosovo and Serbia so far is not strictly speaking an ethnic one. Many of the Serbs of Kosovo north of the Ibar would like their municipalities to be given back to Serbia. Albanians in the Presevo valley area of southern Serbia would like to join Kosovo. In the summer of 2018, Kosovo President Thaçi took up the cudgels for this idea, which Belgrade has long favored, calling it "border correction." The Americans and Europeans, who in the past had always ruled it out, pronounced themselves ready to consider any proposition Belgrade and Pristina could agree on. Only Chancellor Merkel has opposed the idea vigorously.

Adjusting the lines to accommodate ethnic differences in this way would precipitate, likely sooner but certainly later, the movement of all Serbs out of Kosovo, including the majority who live south of the Ibar, and all the Albanians out of Serbia, including those who do not live in the Albanian-majority municipalities in southern Serbia. Such mass population movements involving more than one hundred thousand people would be particularly unwelcome to the majority of Kosovo Serbs, who live south of the Ibar, and to the Serb Orthodox Church, whose major religious sites would be lost. "Border correction" would also raise questions about the territorial integrity of Macedonia, Bosnia, Montenegro, and Serbia, whose Bosniak population might prefer to join whatever portion of Bosnia the Bosniaks would still control. The result would destabilize the entire region. Keeping the lines where they happen to lie, while encouraging correct treatment of minorities in both Kosovo and Serbia, has proven a viable and judicious approach.

Notes

1. On the prewar history of Kosovo, see Noel Malcolm, *Kosovo: A Short History* (New York: New York University Press, 1998); Tim Judah, *The Serbs: History, Myth, and the Destruction of Yugoslavia* (New Haven:

Yale University Press, 1997). On its path to independence, see, for a European perspective, James Ker-Lindsay, *Kosovo: The Path to Contested Statehood in the Balkans* (London: I. B. Tauris, 2009); for a more American perspective, see David L. Phillips, *Liberating Kosovo: Coercive Diplomacy and U.S. Intervention* (Cambridge: MIT Press, 2012).
2. I know of no reason to believe that future security concerns, as hypothesized by Ahsan I. Butt in *Secession and Security: Explaining State Strategy against Separatists* (Ithaca, NY: Cornell University Press, 2017), factored into Milošević's decision making.
3. Shkelzen Maliqi, *Why Nonviolent Resistance in Kosovo Failed* (Pristina: Revista MM dhe Qendra per Studime Humanistike "Gani Bobi," 2011).
4. Paul Hockenos, *Homeland Calling: Exile Patriotism and the Balkan Wars* (Ithaca: Cornell University Press, 2003).
5. Human Rights Watch, "Kosovo War Crimes Chronology," https://www.hrw.org/legacy/campaigns/kosovo98/timeline.shtml.
6. Daniel Serwer and Lauren van Metre, *Kosovo Dialogue: Too Little, Too Late*, Special Report (Washington, DC: United States Institute of Peace, 1998); Daniel Serwer, "Kosovo's Peace Imperfect," *Washington Times*, October 29, 1998.
7. William Walker, interview, *War in Europe*, Frontline, Public Broadcasting Service, accessed April 5, 2016.
8. Louis Sell, *Slobodan Milosevic and the Destruction of Yugoslavia* (Durham: Duke University Press, 2003), 304–5.
9. Benjamin S. Lambeth, "Why Milošević Gave Up When He Did," in *NATO's Air War for Kosovo: A Strategic and Operational Assessment* (Santa Monica, CA: RAND, 2001), 67–86. Also see James Gow, *The Serbian Project and Its Adversaries: A Strategy of War Crimes* (Montreal: McGill-Queen's University Press).
10. Veton Surroi, *The Gorillas We Didn't See (How They're Destroying the State … and Other Heretical Notes)* (Pristina: Koha, 2017).
11. Lauren Van Metre, Albert Cevallos, and Kristine Herrmann, *Kosovo: Escaping the Cul-de-Sac* (Washington, DC: United States Institute of Peace, 1998).
12. *The Milošević Regime Versus Serbian Democracy and Balkan Stability: Hearing Before the Commission on Security and Cooperation in Europe, One Hundred Fifth Congress, Second Session, December 10, 1998*, 41. https://www.csce.gov/sites/helsinkicommission.house.gov/files/Official%20Transcript%20-%20MILOSEVIC%20VERSUS%20SERBIAN%20DEMOCRACY%20AND%20BALKAN%20STABILITY.pdf. I have told this story in more detail in "American Support for Serbian Democracy," in *The Balkan Prism: A Retrospective by Policy-Makers and Analysts*, ed. Johana Deimel and Wim van Meurs (Munich: Verlag Otto Sagner, 2007), 291–96.

13. Judge Kevin Parker, *Report to the President: Death of Slobodan Milošević*, May 2006, http://www.icty.org/x/cases/slobodan_milosevic/custom2/en/parkerreport.pdf.
14. Dejan Djokic, "The Assassination of Zoran Đinđić," OpenDemocracy, March 13, 2003, https://www.opendemocracy.net/democracy-yugoslavia/article_1042.jsp.
15. Serbia's Constitution of 2006, https://www.constituteproject.org/constitution/Serbia_2006.pdf.
16. Humanitarian Law Center, "Transitional Justice in Serbia in the Period from 2013 to 2015," http://www.hlc-rdc.org/?p=32161&lang=de.
17. See also my, "Kosovo: An Unlikely Success Still in the Making," Chapter 5 in *Independence Movements and Their Aftermath: Self-Determination and the Struggle for Success*, ed. Jon B. Alterman and Will Todman (Lanham, MD: Rowman & Littlefield, forthcoming 2018).
18. UN Security Council Resolution 1244 (1999), https://peacemaker.un.org/sites/peacemaker.un.org/files/990610_SCR1244%281999%29.pdf; and Military Technical Agreement between the International Security Force ("KFOR") and the Governments of the Federal Republic of Yugoslavia and the Republic of Serbia, https://www.nato.int/kosovo/docu/a990609a.htm.
19. United Nations, "Implementing 'Standard Before Status,' Policy Core Political Project for UN Kosovo Mission," press release, February 2004, https://www.un.org/press/en/2004/sc7999.doc.htm.
20. European Commission, Commission Staff Working Document, *Kosovo* 2015 Report* (Brussels, 2015), 12–13, 59–60, https://ec.europa.eu/neighbourhood-enlargement/sites/near/files/pdf/key_documents/2015/20151110_report_kosovo.pdf.
21. Balkan Analysis, "International Organizations: Kosovo," http://www.balkanalysis.com/kosovo/international-organizations.
22. Valerie Percival and Egbert Sondorp, "A Case Study of Health Sector Reform in Kosovo," *Conflict and Health* 4, no. 7 (2010), https://doi.org/10.1186/1752-1505-4-7.
23. Marc Sommers and Peter Buckland, *Parallel Worlds: Rebuilding the Education System in Kosovo* (Paris: International Institute for Education Planning, 2004).
24. On 2004, see James Ker-Lindsay, *Kosovo: The Path to Contested Statehood in the Balkans* (London: I. B. Tauris, 2009), 20–22. On earlier incidents see Julie Mertus, *Kosovo: How Myths and Truths Started a War* (Berkeley: University of California Press, 1999).
25. Organization for Security and Co-operation in Europe, "Report on the Role of the Media in the March 2004 Events in Kosovo by the OSCE

Representative on Freedom of the Media," April 2004, https://www.osce.org/fom/30265.
26. Kai Eide, "A Comprehensive Review of the Situation in Kosovo," *Official Documents System of the United Nations*, October 7, 2005, https://undocs.org/S/2005/635.
27. For the details of the negotiations, see James Ker-Lindsay, *Kosovo: The Path to Contested Statehood in the Balkans* (London: I. B. Tauris, 2009).
28. Marc Weller, "The Vienna Negotiations on the Final Status of Kosovo," *International Affairs* 84, no. 4 (2008): 659–81, https://doi.org/10.1111/j.1468-2346.2008.00731.x and "Kosovo's Final Status," 84, no. 6 (2008): 1223–43, https://doi.org/10.1111/j.1468-2346.2008.00766.x.
29. Martti Ahtisaari, *Report of the Special Envoy of the Secretary-General on Kosovo's Future Status*, OSCE, 2007, https://www.osce.org/kosovo/24787?download=true.
30. International Civilian Office, *State Building and Exit: The International Civilian Office and Kosovo's Supervised Independence, 2008–2012* (Pristina: ICO, 2012), https://doi.org/10.4324/9780203964712.
31. Andrea Lorenzo Capussela, *State-Building in Kosovo: Democracy, Corruption and the EU in the Balkans* (London: I. B. Tauris, 2015).
32. Dušan Janjić, "Normalization Challenges: Analysis of the Negotiation Process and the Implementation of the Brussels Agreement" (Belgrade: Forum for Ethnic Relations Policy Paper, 2015), http://fer.org.rs/wp-content/uploads/2017/12/107-FORUM-Policy-Paper-2015-ENG.pdf; Assembly of the Republic of Kosovo, "Law No. 04/L-199 on Ratification of the First International Agreement of Principles Governing the Normalization of Relations between the Republic of Kosovo and the Republic of Serbia," June 27, 2013, https://www.kuvendikosoves.org/common/docs/ligjet/Law%20on%20ratification%20of%20agreement%20-normalization%20of%20relations%20between%20Kosovo%20and%20Serbia.pdf.
33. Surroi, *The Gorillas We Didn't See*.
34. Robert Muharremi, "Kosovo Security Force Is an Army: Legal Arguments," (Kosovar Centre for Security Studies Policy Brief), March 2016, http://www.qkss.org/en/Policy-Papers/Kosovo-Security-Force-is-an-Army-Legal-Arguments-649.
35. For the much more complicated real story, see Stephen D. Krasner, *Sovereignty: Organized Hypocrisy* (Princeton: Princeton University Press, 1999).
36. Accordance with International Law of the Unilateral Declaration of Independence in Respect of Kosovo, Advisory Opinion (I.C.J. Reports 2010), 403, http://www.icj-cij.org/files/case-related/141/141-20100722-ADV-01-00-EN.pdf.

90   D. SERWER

Open Access This chapter is distributed under the terms of the Creative Commons Attribution 4.0 International License (http://creativecommons.org/licenses/by/4.0/), which permits use, duplication, adaptation, distribution and reproduction in any medium or format, as long as you give appropriate credit to the original author(s) and the source, a link is provided to the Creative Commons license and any changes made are indicated.

The images or other third party material in this chapter are included in the work's Creative Commons license, unless indicated otherwise in the credit line; if such material is not included in the work's Creative Commons license and the respective action is not permitted by statutory regulation, users will need to obtain permission from the license holder to duplicate, adapt or reproduce the material.

CHAPTER 6

Can the Balkans Join the West?

Abstract Today, the Balkans—even the enduring trouble spots in Bosnia, Macedonia, Serbia, and Kosovo—are at peace. The region struggled through a violent post-Communist decade in the 1990s but in the early years of the new millennium made real progress in transitioning to more open, democratic societies. Balkans trade and finance are already linked to European markets, but the EU has stalled enlargement until 2025, when it intends to be ready to welcome additional Balkan members. Montenegro and Serbia lead the regatta, but both face major challenges in institutionalizing the rule of law. That is even more true of the laggards, Bosnia and Kosovo. While skepticism about qualifications and dates is justified, the incentive of EU membership is vital to driving continued reform in the region.

Keywords EU and NATO enlargement · Russia · Rule of law · Transitional justice · Corruption · State capture

Balkan peace and security has been a joint European and American enterprise since the NATO intervention in Bosnia in 1995. Though often at odds on specific issues, Americans and Europeans have worked in tandem on Dayton implementation, conflict prevention and resolution in Macedonia, the failed negotiations at Rambouillet, democratization in Serbia, and state-building in Kosovo. While the United States has often taken the military and diplomatic lead, Europe has just as often paid the lion's share of the bills and provided most of the military and civilian personnel. Experience suggests that when Brussels and Washington act in tandem, the odds of success are high.

This cooperation is now based on a common understanding that the countries of the Balkans belong in European and Euro-Atlantic institutions, including NATO if they want to join. That has meant they should all be democratic states with market economies governed under the rule of law. This is an ambitious work in progress, under difficult conditions. Progress is slow but palpable. Bulgaria and Romania, untouched by war in the 1990s, entered NATO in 2004 and the EU in 2007. Croatia and Albania joined NATO in 2009. Croatia joined the EU in 2013. Montenegro joined NATO in 2017. Macedonia is ready for NATO membership once the name issue with Greece is resolved. Montenegro and Serbia are trying to qualify for EU membership by 2023, which is necessary to accede in 2025, after two years required for ratifications by the member states. This is a record of success, not failure, even if the process is slower than many might like.

There is one sense in which the Balkans are already imbued with the EU. The euro is either used in circulation or as a peg by all the countries of former Yugoslavia except Serbia. The benighted currency that many blame for Europe's current malaise has great virtue in the Balkans. Use of the euro has removed inflation and budgetary licentiousness as options for Balkan politicians. They have no option to devalue and no seigniorage (profits from producing currency), as they cannot print or mint euros. The result is an unexpected level of financial virtue in a region unlikely to develop it organically, as well as a reduction in frictional costs associated with currency exchange.

Good as it may be from those perspectives, the euro's problems and the lengthy European recession (lasting from 2008 to 2013), followed by slow growth, depressed not only Balkan economies but also spirits. Even today, many observers see little more than doom and gloom in the Balkans.[1] Some think the post-Yugoslav peace settlements are on the verge of unraveling and would like to redraw borders along ethnic lines, imagining that could somehow be done without war.[2] It is common today for people who live in the Balkans to suggest that they were better off under Tito in Socialist Yugoslavia, an allegation that neither honest memory nor per capita GDP figures support. Growth has been slower since the 1990s wars than prior to them, and both growth and institutional reform have lagged the pace the Baltics and Eastern Europe set after 1989.[3] The per capita GDP gap with more developed countries is not narrowing. But all the former Yugoslav republics and Kosovo have seen substantial gains in per capita GDP, without counting their still substantial gray-market economies. Except in Kosovo, the "misery index" (unemployment plus inflation) improved throughout former Yugoslavia until 2010, when the global financial crisis hit the region hard.[4] Looking forward, the World Bank sees resilient growth in the Balkans as well as improvement in employment and poverty reduction, albeit with rising risks.[5]

The temporary exigencies of the business cycle should not, however, distract from the region's long-run prospects. Can the Balkans ever really be part of the West? Will the region's war-torn and still troubled states abide by European values, enjoy European standards of living, and contribute to European peace and security? Can the countries that want to do so manage to equip themselves to join NATO and the EU?

The answers are not only up to those who live in and lead the Balkan states. Europe is suffering a crisis of confidence, enlargement fatigue, and nativist resurgence, brought on by recession, financial instability precipitated by the Greek debt crisis, the less-than-stellar post-accession performance of Bulgaria and Romania in implementing the rule of law, and waves of migration from North Africa and the Middle East, flowing in part through the Balkans. The UK's Brexit referendum in June 2016 cast a pall of doubt over Balkan EU aspirations. Poland and Hungary, which after the Berlin Wall fell were paradigms of liberal democratic transformation, are displaying troubling populist and authoritarian tendencies, as is Croatia.[6] Even the territorial integrity of some existing EU members is in question: the independence aspirations of Scotland and Catalonia have made several EU countries nervous and less friendly than ever to Kosovo.

More broadly, the West is no longer the solid pillar of liberal democratic aspirations that it once was. President Trump has questioned NATO's mutual defense commitment, especially to Montenegro, casting doubts on the Alliance's usefulness and durability. American "national security" tariffs on steel and aluminum as well as the unilateral withdrawal from the Iran nuclear deal have offended Europe, Canada, and Japan. President Trump has also said he regards Europe as an economic foe and appears unaware of the partnership with Europe that has been at least partly successful in the Balkans. Ethnic nationalism is no longer only a Balkans syndrome: it is apparent throughout the EU and in the United

States. The "West" as a liberal democratic construct is in peril as Russia takes advantage of opportunities to rattle its foundations while rapidly growing China rises as a strategic competitor.

Is it realistic to imagine that the door to the West really will open? Or that the West will remain a bastion of democracy? Has EU enlargement fatigue become enlargement exhaustion? Can the United States and the EU maintain their tandem efforts in the Balkans even as tension grows between Brussels and Washington? Will the remaining non-EU Balkan countries end up like Turkey, a NATO member but an eternal aspirant on the EU's periphery, sliding toward autocracy? Or will they not even get into NATO but remain on the periphery of both the EU and the Alliance?

Russia is now a key negative factor in the Euro-Atlantic ambitions of some Balkan countries. Orthodox Slavs in the Balkans have cultural, linguistic, religious, and historical ties to Russia. More religious and nationalist Serbs (in Serbia, Bosnia, and Montenegro) as well as some Macedonians feel the strong pull of Orthodox solidarity. Serbs have not forgotten the NATO bombings suffered during the Bosnia and Kosovo Wars. While Yeltsin's Russia in the 1990s was preoccupied with its own problems and unable to project image or power even as far as the Balkans, Putin's Russia is intervening militarily in Ukraine and Syria and is supplying major weapons systems to Serbia as well as equipment and training to Serb police in both Serbia and Bosnia. Putin's dominance in his July 2018 public appearance with President Trump in Helsinki will reinforce for some in the Balkans the idea that liberal democracy is fading while ethnic nationalism and Slavic solidarity are rising.

Moscow is doing what it can to exploit its pan-Slavic hard and soft power in the Balkans, with the objective of preventing NATO membership for Macedonia in the near term and eventually for Bosnia and Serbia.[7] The means are many.[8] Russian energy supplies, loans, organized crime, cyberattacks, and cultural and religious connections all serve the Kremlin's purposes.[9] Moscow promotes demonstrations against NATO, talks up Russia's role in the world and downplays NATO's, invites lots of Slav officials and politicians to visit, conducts military exercises with Serbia, and has established a "humanitarian" logistics base there. Russian companies have invested in Serbia, Montenegro, and the Republika Srpska part of Bosnia.[10] *Russia Today* and *Sputnik News* feed the Balkans media nationalist and anti-Western stories.

These anti-NATO efforts have strengthened significantly in recent years.[11] Most notably, in October 2016, Moscow campaigned against Montenegro's pro-NATO prime minister, supplying funds and organization to his principal opponent, and set in motion a coup plot to enable pro-Russian politicians there to seize power in the event they lost the election. Only the cooperation of Serbia's prime minister and quick action by the Montenegrin security services prevented the Russian-linked plotters from killing Prime Minister Đukanović.[12] The United States' November 2016 election was not the only one President Putin tried to disrupt.

Will Macedonia be prepared to buck Russia's growing opposition to NATO membership, as Montenegro has? Will Bosnia achieve the kind of cross-ethnic consensus to allow it to ask for a NATO Membership Action Plan? Will Serbia, Bosnia, Macedonia, and Kosovo be able and willing to institute the political and economic reforms needed for EU accession?

The idea of *all* the Balkans countries eventually joining the EU and NATO is a recent and daring one. Europe in the 1990s was still thinking of the Balkans countries as a neighborhood issue, not membership possibilities. NATO regarded the Balkans as "out of area" until it intervened in Bosnia in 1995. While individuals may have imagined such a development earlier, and Slovenia was already well on its way soon after independence in 1991, the origin of the idea of a Euro-Atlantic destination for *all* the Balkans can be traced to the Sarajevo Summit of 1999, which launched an initiative called the Stability Pact. It sought to engage the region in mutually beneficial efforts of many different sorts, from human rights to free trade and from energy supply to fighting organized crime.[13]

Whatever the merits of the specific projects undertaken by the Stability Pact, which today has been transformed into a Regional Cooperation Council focused mainly on infrastructure, jobs, and other economic issues, it represented the dawn of one big idea: those Balkan countries that want to do so could prepare for and hope to enter the EU, other European organizations like the Council of Europe and the European Investment Bank, as well as NATO. This idea was codified at the 2003 Thessaloniki EU Summit: "The EU reiterates its unequivocal support to the European perspective of the Western Balkan countries. The future of the Balkans is within the European Union."[14] This teleological postulate is extraordinary. Just eight years after the war in Bosnia, just four after the war in Kosovo, and just three after the fall of Milošević, the EU declared its willingness to accept *all* the countries of the Western

Balkans as members, if they qualify. Those eligible for EU membership are normally regarded as eligible also for NATO membership. No one should minimize this development, which gave at least some in the Balkans a clear sense of direction and purpose during the first decade of this century.

NATO membership has proven easier and quicker to qualify for than EU membership, though delays in accession are still common. Slovenia, Croatia, and Albania are already NATO members. Montenegro failed to get in at the Wales Summit in 2014 mainly because the Alliance did not want to take the risk of provoking an already overwrought Russia, which had invaded Ukraine, for an infinitesimal gain in Alliance military capability. Rebuffing Moscow's entreaties, inducements, and threats, Podgorica received an invitation at the NATO Summit in Warsaw in 2016 and formally entered in 2017. Macedonia is now fully qualified. It got an invitation to join NATO in July 2018, with accession likely a year later, provided the name issue is resolved.

For now, Belgrade is not seeking NATO membership, but it has joined Partnership for Peace, the NATO anteroom for non-members, and frequently joins NATO exercises and training activities. Russia, however, will work hard in Serbia against NATO, as it did in Montenegro. Putin's annexation of Crimea and invasion of eastern Ukraine have revived the hopes of some in Belgrade that Serbia might be able to achieve something similar in Kosovo, annexing or at least de facto controlling the Serb-majority territory in the north. Some also harbor hopes of Republika Srpska seceding from Bosnia. If those are your objectives, you would lean over backwards to befriend Moscow.

Kosovo has a wide social consensus in favor of NATO membership among the Albanians, but it lacks an army. Its lightly armed security forces focus on emergency relief and leave the defense of its territory mostly to KFOR. The Americans and Europeans are insisting that Pristina make a concerted effort to gain Kosovo Serb approval for its creation, but that is proving impossible due to Belgrade's opposition. Kosovo will build its armed forces to NATO standards from the start, likely relying on legislation rather than a constitutional amendment.[15] So long as Pristina can ensure that its neighbors do not get nervous about its capabilities, the route to NATO's Partnership for Peace could be blessedly short. The only real obstacle to membership is the presence inside the Alliance of four members that do not yet recognize Kosovo: Spain, Greece, Romania, and Slovakia.

Kosovo will need a security force able to counter a Serbian invasion for at least a week or ten days, as well as an ironclad agreement with NATO for help should Serbia move to retake any part of Kosovo's territory. You only need watch what Russia has done in Ukraine, Georgia, and Moldova, or remember what Serb forces did in Croatia, Bosnia, and Kosovo in the 1990s, to recognize how important it is to be able to protect the borders of a state that claims to be sovereign. By the same token, Serbian recognition and exchange of ambassadors would alleviate the threat and allow Kosovo to build less potent forces more adapted to international deployments, which are a main activity for the Croatian, Albanian, Montenegrin, and Macedonian armed forces because there is no serious remaining threat at home.

Bosnia is divided on NATO, as it is on many things. Its Serb leadership shows little interest in the Alliance, which contributed mightily to the defeat of Republika Srpska's army at the end of the war in 1995 and helped force the unification of Bosnia's three armies a decade later. The Alliance wants issues arising from the division of military property in Bosnia resolved before it will give Bosnia a plan for achieving membership. But entering NATO, like EU membership, would mean a strengthened central government in Sarajevo, which would displease Republika Srpska's President Dodik as well as the country's more nationalist Croat leadership. It is therefore convenient for them to hold tough on the defense property issues, as they have for years. Today's small Bosnian Army might readily meet NATO standards, as it has worked closely with the Alliance for more than ten years. Bosnia's Muslims and many of its secularists would welcome NATO membership, but it would require nationalist Serb and Croat political support that for now is lacking.

EU membership is far more difficult than NATO membership and takes much longer. Why? All aspirants for EU membership need to be able to implement the *acquis communautaire*, the body of law and regulation that enables an EU member to be an EU member. There is no way to summarize its now thirty-five chapters. Standing on a street corner in Rome, the *acquis* surrounds you: it requires the newly made curb cuts, it determines the shape, size, and graphics on the street signs, it dictates the sanitary standards in the restaurants and markets as well as the fiduciary requirements for the banks.

In addition to these technical standards, Balkan countries need to undertake the political and economic reforms required for them to qualify, a bar that rises with every new enlargement. For the states emerging from former Yugoslavia, the transformation is a multi-faceted one: from state-centered socialism to free-market capitalism, from autocracy to liberal democracy, from war to peace, from ethnic nationalism that privileges one group over others to respect for minorities and individual human rights, and from corrupt cronyism to transparent and accountable governance. However attractive in theory, such transformations threaten domestic elites and traditional patronage networks, which resist. The EU uses conditionality to try to overcome such resistance. Financing, technical assistance, and infrastructure investments depend on progress in meeting EU requirements. But that effort is a complex and difficult one whose impact depends on the domestic conditions in each prospective member, including most notably the degree to which the state is well established and uncontested both internally and externally.[16] The history of the former Yugoslav states since 2003 revolves in large part around the successes and failures of this effort to build states that can qualify for EU membership, which is still far from completed.

The contrast with the previous decade is striking. In 1991 the Luxembourgeois politician Jacques Poos had declared that "the hour of Europe has dawned" on his way to the negotiation that ended the war in Slovenia. He meant that Europe would peacefully end war in the Balkans, not that the Balkans would ever join Europe. That statement was the object of derision for years in the State Department as Europe's persistent but futile efforts to bring the Balkan wars to a close failed miserably in Croatia, Bosnia, and Kosovo. American diplomats often referred to the Europeans laughingly with the f-word: feckless. Today, however, Washington sees EU and NATO membership for those Balkan countries that qualify as a serious, even indispensable objective, not least because it at least partially relieves Washington of what might otherwise be a burden. Washington has tried to pass leadership in the Balkans to the EU.[17]

The EU's willingness to open its doors to the Western Balkans has had an extraordinary impact in those countries most able to take advantage of the opportunity. Slovenia entered the EU in 2004. Croatia in the first decade of this century made a concerted effort to prepare itself for EU membership, and in 2013 it succeeded. Montenegro and Serbia are now leading the regatta for EU membership and show substantial signs of getting serious about efforts to qualify. The EU invented a "high-level dialogue" for Macedonia that was intended to substitute for the accession negotiations Greece would not allow, but that bureaucratic exercise failed to convince Macedonia's citizens and leadership that EU membership was a realistic objective. It is hard to maintain political momentum to adopt often burdensome EU requirements when candidacy appears unattainable. But Albania and Macedonia are now slated to start negotiations before the end of 2019, provided the former meets EU demands concerning corruption and rule of law and the latter succeeds in its effort to resolve the name issue with Greece. The lessons learned in the premature 2007 accessions of Bulgaria and Romania are being applied.[18]

Serbia formally started EU accession negotiations in January 2014. Belgrade got candidacy status and later the date for negotiations to begin not strictly on the traditional merits but rather as a reward for progress in normalization of relations with Pristina, consummated in the April 2013 Brussels Agreement that provided for reintegration of the northern Serb-majority municipalities with the rest of Kosovo. Many in Washington and Brussels felt that it was more important to get Serbia into the process than to insist on all the preconditions, which reduce the attractiveness and immediacy of EU membership and thereby diminish the incentives for reform. In December 2015, Serbia opened Chapter 35, which includes normalization of relations with Kosovo, and Chapter 32, on financial controls.

Belgrade is certainly serious about the EU but is still not fully aligned with it, especially in foreign policy. President Vučić has deemphasized holding on to all of Kosovo, without, however, promising bilateral recognition. Though he knows it, he does not publicly acknowledge that EU members that have recognized Kosovo will not accept Serbia as a member if it continues to claim sovereignty. Serbia remains at odds with the EU over press freedom and has refused to align its positions with Brussels on Ukraine, sanctions on Russia, and the (now cancelled) Putin-sponsored South Stream natural gas pipeline. Some in Serbia pride themselves even after the end of the Cold War on leadership in the Non-Aligned Movement. The EU knows a great deal about dealing with issues of this sort. Sweden, Finland, and Austria all saw themselves as "neutral" during their accession to the EU, but that occurred in 1993 at a much less contentious time in relations between the West and Moscow. Serbia's reluctance to defy Moscow could slow the accession process, assuming current tensions between the EU and Russia over Ukraine continue.[19]

The two remaining laggards in joining the EU are Bosnia and Kosovo. In Kosovo, both elite and grassroots verbal support for EU membership is strong. All its legislation is required to be consistent with EU standards, although implementation often lags shamefully.[20] Also important is that Europe is divided on Kosovo's independence, with five EU members not yet recognizing Kosovo. This split renders the EU less than enthusiastic about making Kosovo a candidate and opening an accession negotiation with Pristina. Kosovo's leadership doubts that the EU can deliver on membership, but Kosovo signed a Stabilization and Association Agreement with the EU in 2015 and has qualified for a visa waiver program, which all other Balkan countries already have.

In Bosnia, elite support for EU membership is weak and grassroots interest is flagging. Its politicians appear to be suffering the "Sanader effect." Several no doubt fear that the more independent judiciary and stronger anti-corruption efforts the EU requires would land them in jail. Getting into the visa waiver program for Europe's Schengen Area did mobilize Sarajevo to quick action to meet European passport standards, but in general Bosnia has lagged in meeting European requirements. The British and Germans initiated in 2014 an effort to do for Sarajevo what was done for Belgrade: give it an easy ticket to candidacy status, provided the Bosnians adopt minimal reforms to the country's labor laws in preparation for privatization. The Europeans think this will reduce corruption, make the carrot of EU membership more imminently attractive, and allow the European Commission to wield the stick more forcefully during the accession negotiations rather than in anticipation of them. This approach would cost Europe some credibility in the short term, but those who advocate it think it will increase the pressure on Balkans politicians to ignore the Sanader effect and run the risks associated with the EU accession process. So far, it has not worked.[21] Bosnia submitted a membership application to the EU in 2016 and managed to respond to the EU's questionnaire about its qualifications by early 2018, but its answers demonstrated all too clearly that it still lacks the internal cohesion and state capacity required to make a serious run at accession.[22]

It has been argued that Europe's transformational power has met its match in postwar Balkan environments, especially in Bosnia and Kosovo.[23] Certainly no one would argue that their accession is inevitable, despite the decades that have passed since their conflicts. Backsliding happens, due principally to weak institutions and authoritarian political bosses.[24] Nor, however, is it clear that their transformations are destined for ultimate failure. In Bosnia the problem is nationalist leadership that relies on the current constitutional framework to ensure their hold on power. They have no need to deliver political or economic reform to satisfy their ethnically defined constituencies. A trans-ethnic challenge could, however, be mounted, either at the ballot box or in the streets, especially if it finds support in both Brussels and Washington. If that happens, Bosnia could advance quickly toward both NATO and the EU, as happened in Macedonia after the fall of Gruevski. In Kosovo the main diplomatic issue is incomplete sovereignty, which could be resolved in negotiations Brussels reinitiated in July 2018. Kosovo need not remain a case of contested statehood, and it will not if Belgrade gets serious about EU membership, which will require recognition and establishment of diplomatic relations with its former province. The dire consequences of allowing Kosovo's status to remain unresolved are all too foreseeable.[25]

For both Bosnia and Kosovo, divisions within the West are a large part of what makes EU and NATO accession so difficult and their "transformational" impact so dilute. Closing those divisions would go a long way toward increasing the incentive of Sarajevo and Pristina to hasten reforms. In Bosnia, what is needed is for the United States and the EU to agree on minimal constitutional reforms that would enable all citizens to be candidates for the presidency and empower the Sarajevo government with the authority it needs to negotiate and implement the *acquis communautaire*. In Kosovo, what is needed is for the five EU members who do not recognize Kosovo's sovereignty (Cyprus, Greece, Romania, Slovakia, and Spain) to commit to doing so once it qualifies for EU candidacy. Even if two or three would do so, the effect would be significant. Greece—once it has settled the name issue with Macedonia—Romania, and Slovakia have no strong basis on which to continue to deny recognition. Spain and Cyprus do so for fear it might encourage the independence ambitions of Catalonia and Northern Cyprus. That is specious, unless they regard their own governments as the moral equivalent of Milošević's Serbia.

Perhaps the most difficult part of qualifying for EU membership is respect for individual human rights, which is at the core of what defines liberal democratic regimes. Nowhere in the territory that once belonged to Yugoslavia is commitment to human rights at truly European levels, though Slovenia comes closest. The other former Yugoslav states have all gone through a process of denial of human rights violations, lip service to human rights norms, tactical concessions on relatively minor issues like display of flags, as well as avowed and legislated but often still hollow commitment to meeting EU standards. While many observers bemoan the lack of sincerity, this happens to correspond to the "spiral model" of adaptation of autocracies to international human rights norms.[26] None of the former Yugoslav states have entirely internalized them or complied in detail with their requirements, largely because there is little domestic constituency insisting that they do so, except among abused minorities. The committed and energetic civil society organizations that advocate for human rights throughout the Balkans have limited mass appeal. Nor have any of the former Yugoslav states become serious promoters of human rights norms internationally, except when applied to their co-ethnics across the border (Serbs in Croatia, for example, or Bosniaks in Serbia). Those are future stages of the "spiral model," which will require another decade or more.

One of the key barriers to completing this process of adaptation to human rights norms is accountability for past atrocities, known these days as "transitional justice." There are still individuals, ideologies, and institutions in the Balkans associated with wartime abuses. Bosnia's Republika Srpska was originally founded to create a Serb-dominated area cleansed of Croats and Bosniaks that would eventually unify with Serbia. The winning political party in Croatia's 2016 parliamentary election played an important role in trying to create a Croat entity in Bosnia during the Bosniak/Croat war and in advocating ethnic cleansing of Serbs in 1995. Two of Kosovo's main political parties (and its current president and prime minister) trace their origins to the Kosovo Liberation Army, which committed abuses against both Serbs and Albanians during and after the 1999 war. Serbia's president and foreign minister were associated with the Milošević regime in the 1990s.

We are still a long way from the sincere mutual acknowledgment of harm that is known to enable a spiral of genuine reconciliation.[27] The International Criminal Court for the former Yugoslavia captured all and tried most of its 161 indictees, including major wartime leaders, and domestic courts have prosecuted lower-level perpetrators, especially in Serbia and Bosnia. The removal of high-level indicted war criminals from their home countries was vital. Had they remained, either free or under arrest, they would have made governance and democratization even harder than it has been.[28] But many indictees are still regarded as heroes in their home countries. Acquittals of co-nationals are greeted with joy and convictions with resentment. Apologies often ring hollow. Higher-level indictments in domestic courts lag, and none of the trials has had a truly transformative effect on public opinion or domestic norms.[29] A grassroots civil society campaign for a regional truth and reconciliation commission has not yet been successful.[30] Especially in Serbia, whose wartime leader was so instrumental to the wars of Yugoslav succession, the outcome so far is a shifting discourse on guilt, responsibility, and denial that is at best partial, ambiguous, or both.[31]

The hardest part of qualifying for both the EU and NATO is rule of law, which appears in several of the chapters (especially 23 and 24) and is an indispensable foundation for the whole. The all too obvious failure of EU members Romania and Bulgaria to meet European rule-of-law standards before accession caused Brussels to stiffen its requirements and initiate negotiation of rule-of-law issues early in the process, since they take a long time to resolve. Accession for Slovenia and Croatia was challenging, but the remaining non-member Balkans countries will face a still harder road.

This is a good thing, not a bad one. Serbia, Montenegro, Albania, Kosovo, Macedonia, and Bosnia will all have problems meeting European rule-of-law standards, but doing so will benefit each of them immensely. Foreign and domestic investors, as well as ordinary citizens, want to know that they will be treated fairly, which requires a capable and transparent system of laws and courts. They also want to know their money and property will not be stolen.

The two biggest rule-of-law issues throughout the Balkans are corruption and inter-ethnic crime. Both require not only good laws on the books but also good implementation. Corruption in the United States is generally defined as the abuse of public office for private gain. The opposite of corruption is not anti-corruption. It is good governance: the use of public office for public gain. That depends not only on good laws, good courts, and a good anti-corruption agency but also on social norms, free media, political competition, independent regulatory institutions, and vigorous civil society.

Balkan governments pass good laws and create anti-corruption agencies. What they lack are the other elements. This puts most Balkan countries around the second quartile of the global 2017 Transparency International Corruptions Perceptions rankings.[32] This is not good, though Romania, Bulgaria, and Greece—already EU members—are in this range as well. No one in the Balkans is immune. Corruption is a regional problem, derived in part from wartime smuggling and sanctions-busting on all sides as well as persistent family connections that make nepotism in hiring not only common but expected. Low public-sector salaries, overly powerful political parties, and weak professionalism among government workers contribute as well. The Communist states in the Balkans may have looked strong before the fall of the Berlin Wall, but in fact they were fragile and all too often incompetent. Autocracy betokened weakness, not strength.

What does this mean for the region's citizens? Close to 10% of Kosovo's population pays bribes every year.[33] That might not sound like a lot, but if we assume it has been going on since independence and it is not always the same people paying bribes, most of the population has paid a bribe, and the others will have heard about it and likely soon do it. That creates a culture of impunity. Corruption is not only about the trash collector, the building permit, and the business license. Some high-level malfeasance is invisible. But there is also malfeasance that is apparent in the way people live, entertain, and behave. If government officials are living beyond their means, consorting with known criminals or hiring their relatives, it is usually no big secret. What is needed are courageous journalists who will write about it, newspapers that will publish it, civil society organizations that will campaign against it, and voters who will cast their ballots with it in mind. And then prosecutors and judges who will investigate, prosecute, and convict.

One form of corruption much discussed throughout the Balkans is state capture. This refers to a situation in which private interests control and exploit governments. The implicit comparison is often with fully consolidated democracies, or even with some ideal paragon of democracy.[34] By comparison, the Balkans is highly dependent on political party bosses and their patronage networks, some of which have entrenched themselves for decades. Their clientelist networks know well how to resist, and adapt to, whatever the EU tries to impose. Partitocracy limits the EU's transformative power, enabling formal compliance while blocking serious reform and allowing corrupt practices to continue.[35] Not surprisingly, this is especially the case where domestic accountability—through either autonomous government institutions or civil society—is lacking.[36]

State capture is often blamed on foreigners, especially on the United States and the EU, who are said to prefer a promise of stability even if it means maintaining corrupt leaders in power. The neologism is "stabilitocracy": "Governments that claim to secure stability, pretend to espouse EU integration and rely on informal, clientelist structures, control of the media, and the regular production of crises to undermine democracy and the rule of law."[37] In return for the pretense of stability, the EU is said to pretend to keep the doors open to membership. The implication is that everyone is happy to slow EU accession. There is one clear case: Bosnia, where the EU has purposefully avoided constitutional reforms (over the objections of the United States) that it fears might destabilize the peace settlement. Even in that instance, however, the Russian role in guaranteeing support to Republika Srpska is a key factor that inhibits a forceful effort by the Americans and Europeans. Why try something that is not going to work?

Otherwise, there is little evidence of Western support for such governance, provided there is a viable alternative. In Macedonia, the United States and the EU were prepared to pry the state loose from Prime Minister Gruevski's tight hold, once protesters signaled overwhelming citizen disapproval and electoral results opened up the possibility of a reform-minded democratic alternative. In Albania and Kosovo, the EU and the United States have invested heavily in trying to create independent judiciaries, without much success. Autonomous institutions and civil society there are still weak, but no one in Washington or Brussels is going to be too upset if the judiciaries start indicting current leaders based on real evidence. The constitutional court in Kosovo has intervened more than once to nullify presidential elections, with international backing. There was some regret but little hesitation when Kosovo Prime Minister Hardinaj was shipped to The Hague in 2005. In Montenegro there is still no remotely acceptable alternative to Đukanović, who wins elections without controlling the media against an opposition that opposes the country's independence. By contrast, in Serbia Vučić's media dominance is complete and his opposition too fragmented and weak to present a serious alternative. Concern about "stabilitocracy" supported by Brussels and Washington may not reflect so much the situation in the Balkans as it does European and American dissatisfaction with election results, which often return nationalist heroes and would-be autocrats rather than committed reformers. The disappointment is understandable but ill behooves those advocating democracy.

The people best placed to undo state capture are not the foreigners but a country's own citizens. The problem is arguably that anti-corruption campaigns do not bring electoral success but instead delegitimize elites and destabilize the political system. Citizens do not perceive the corresponding benefits.[38] Foreign governments can and should weigh in to sanction corrupt individuals and human rights violators, using tools like the U.S. Global Magnitsky Act.[39] The EU and its member states have been far too shy about following the U.S. lead in this respect, in part for fear of judicial challenges. But no foreigner knows the Balkans better than the people who live there. It was Italian magistrates like Giovanni Falcone who beat the Sicilian mafia, which murdered him on its way to defeat. Only Italians could do it, though the Americans helped with intelligence and witness protection. It will be courageous Kosovars, Serbs, Bosnians, and Montenegrins who uproot corruption, both at the retail and leadership levels. The EU could certainly help more than it currently does with intelligence, witness protection, and targeted sanctions, but there is no foreign substitute for local courage and conviction.

The same is true of inter-ethnic crime. This has also been much discussed in Kosovo, as the weaknesses of the Kosovo judicial system inspired the internationals to demand a "special court" to try war crimes cases against leaders of the KLA (involving murders of Albanians as well as Serbs and possibly others). The new tribunal is a Kosovo court with international judges and prosecutors convening in The Hague. There is nothing terrible about this proposition. If a Scottish court can convene in The Hague to try the Libyan Pan Am 103 bombers, why can't a Kosovo court? Kosovars, Serbs, and others have been tried by international prosecutors and judges at the International Criminal Tribunal for former Yugoslavia. A Kosovo court with international staff is not an unreasonable proposition to establish accountability and provide a modicum of justice.

"Why us?" people in the Balkans always ask. Other Balkan countries have not been asked to do this, that, or the other thing. Kosovo was asked to establish a special court outside the country because the internationals do not have confidence in the Kosovo courts, not even as much confidence as they have in the Bosnian, Macedonian, and Serbian courts, all of which have made some progress in handling inter-ethnic crime. This should be a source of embarrassment, and inspiration. Enabling the Kosovo courts to deal effectively with inter-ethnic crime should be the goal of anyone wanting Kosovo to be fully sovereign, which is what is required before it can become a EU member.

In addition to corruption and inter-ethnic crime, a third rule-of-law issue threatens to lengthen the process of preparing Bosnia and Kosovo for NATO and EU membership: the recruitment of Islamic State fighters in their generally moderate Muslim populations. The absolute numbers are small: a few hundred fighters from Kosovo, and fewer than that from Bosnia. But relative to population the proportions are high, the highest per capita in Europe.[40] There is no doubt about the willingness of the dominant political parties in both countries to take action—their politicians feel the threat of the Islamic State as strongly as the United States or Europe does. Laws have been passed, but like so much legislation in the Balkans it has proven difficult to implement effectively, and no one has yet figured out what to do with returning foreign fighters.

Improvement in inter-ethnic relations, establishment of rule of law, and blocking recruitment of foreign fighters requires something else that the Balkans still lacks, more than twenty-five years after the fall of the Berlin Wall: economic reform. Throughout the Balkans, people of all ethnicities tell the joke about a farmer (usually of another ethnicity than the storyteller) who finds a magic lantern. When he rubs it and the genie emerges, the farmer's first wish is that his neighbor's cow should die. "What good will that do you?" the genie asks. "None," says the farmer, "but it will make him very unhappy." Sad to say, people in the Balkans laugh at this joke, while admitting it reflects a zero-sum mentality common among all the ethnic groups.

Everyone assumes that a bigger slice means less for someone else. No one has confidence that the pie can be made to grow. Politicians therefore look for international support wherever they can get it: witness opaque loans from Russia to Republika Srpska.[41] Ethnic tension and fat loans help ethnic nationalists stay in power. So too do state-owned companies, which provide patronage and corruption opportunities. One of the keys to further progress throughout the Western Balkans is internationally supervised, transparent privatization.

Renewed economic growth would open new opportunities for youth, ease ethnic tensions, strengthen pro-European political forces, and allow everyone to enjoy his neighbor's prosperity. This is where enterprises like the Regional Cooperation Council, the European Investment Bank, and the European Bank for Reconstruction and Development really count. Goran Svilanović, who as foreign minister happens to have been one of the first Serbian officials to acknowledge that Kosovo was lost, now heads the Regional Cooperation Council, the Balkans-owned heir of the

Stability Pact. Its 2020 South East Europe Strategy, "Jobs and Prosperity in a European Perspective," is precisely what the region needs: its targets are increased trade and investment, growth and jobs, business creation, and improved governance.[42]

Infrastructure is the heart of matter. The road from Durres (Albania) to Pristina is one of the few major improvements in the Balkans transportation infrastructure in the past twenty years. Kosovo spent a great deal of money on it, but it has had no serious positive economic impact. Extension of the road to Nis (in Serbia) would greatly increase its benefits, but of course that is still difficult given rocky Serb/Kosovar relations. That is the kind of effort worth thinking about and working toward in a regional context: it would both make the initial investment worthwhile and could improve inter-ethnic relations.

Vesna Pusić, once Croatia's foreign minister, summarized the first two decades of Croatian independence as moving from heroic to boring politics. Even in Croatia that is not entirely true, as vigorous nationalists have since returned to power there. In Serbia, Bosnia, and Kosovo they have hardly ever left power. There was a heroic moment after the Berlin Wall fell when the most important objectives in fragmented Yugoslavia were the realization of national ambitions, self-determination, and assertion and recognition of national identities and boundaries. Tuđman, Milošević, Izetbegović, Gligorov, and Rugova were the respective national heroes. The better part of their aspirations is fulfilled. Now it is time for the mundane, which Pusić called "boring." Boring and rewarding. The Balkans is no longer at war. Individuals in *specific* places and times may be at risk, which is true in Washington as well as in Mitrovica/Mitrovicë. But no group has reason to fear mass atrocity, and most individuals have no good reason to fear persecution.

Once-oppressed peoples are now majorities or pluralities who should worry less about themselves and more about the minorities who live among them. It will be far easier to meet obligations in that respect in a prosperous environment than in a stagnant one. The Regional Cooperation Council has set reasonable objectives. Meeting them will generate the resources and time needed to work on the far more difficult rule-of-law criteria for EU membership.

The bridge between today and the future of the Balkans in NATO and the EU is paved not with heroism but with political moderation and economic prosperity. Washington and Brussels need to work together to keep the Balkans moving in the right direction, allying with Balkan citizens whenever possible. When they do, no one resists for long. Each Balkan country will need to find its own path. But the vanguard experience of Slovenia, Croatia, Montenegro, and Macedonia points unequivocally in the right direction, even if hesitation and backsliding are frequent. Enlargement fatigue and concern about rule of law have slowed their progress from time to time, and there is never a guarantee that when a country is ready for EU or NATO membership the internal politics of those organizations will align in a way to permit accession. But none of the current or potential Balkan candidates represents more than a tiny fraction of the EU's more than 500 million people (440 million even without the UK). Admitting Bosnia (less than 4 million) or Kosovo (less than 2 million) is not like admitting Turkey's 75 million plus. The trick for each of the Balkans countries is to get ready and wait for the political door to open, which it does from time to time.

If they want, the remaining problem countries of the Balkans—Macedonia, Serbia, Kosovo, and Bosnia—will someday become NATO and EU members. They will also be friends of the United States and leaders in helping the rest of the world find peace and prosperity. That will be a worthy conclusion to more than two decades of intervention. Even opening that possibility has made the effort worthwhile.

Notes

1. For a well-crafted example, see Jasmin Mujanovic, *Hunger and Fury: The Crisis of Democracy in the Balkans* (Oxford: Oxford University Press, 2018).
2. Timothy Less, "Dysfunction in the Balkans: Can the Post-Yugoslav Settlement Survive?" *Foreign Affairs*, December 20, 2016, https://www.foreignaffairs.com/articles/bosnia-herzegovina/2016-12-20/dysfunction-balkans.
3. Oleh Havrylyshyn, Xiaofan Meng, and Marian L. Tupy, "25 Years of Reforms in Ex-communist Countries: Fast and Extensive Reforms Led to Higher Growth and More Political Freedom," *CATO Institute*, no. 795 (July 12, 2016), https://www.cato.org/publications/policy-analysis/25-years-reforms-ex-communist-countries-fast-extensive-reforms-led.
4. Franjo Štiblar, "Economic Growth and Development in Post Yugoslav Countries," Wilson Center Global Europe Program, June 2013, https://www.wilsoncenter.org/sites/default/files/Franjo_Stiblar_WWICS.docx.pdf.
5. World Bank Group, "Resilient Growth Amid Rising Risks," *Southeast Europe Regular Economic Report no. 10* (Fall 2016), http://pubdocs.worldbank.org/en/521981474898709744/SEE-RER-Report-Fall-2016.pdf.

6. Dalibor Rohac, "Hungary and Poland Aren't Democratic: They're Authoritarian," *Foreign Policy*, February 5, 2018, https://foreignpolicy.com/2018/02/05/hungary-and-poland-arent-democratic-theyre-authoritarian/.
7. Margarita Assenova, "Moscow Pushes to Derail Macedonia's NATO Membership," *Eurasia Daily Monitor* 15, no. 117 (August 6, 2018), https://jamestown.org/program/moscow-pushes-to-derail-macedonias-nato-membership/.
8. Mark Galeotti, "Do the Western Balkans Face a Coming Russian Storm?" (European Council on Foreign Relations Policy Brief), April 2018, https://www.ecfr.eu/publications/summary/do_the_western_balkans_face_a_coming_russian_storm.
9. United States Senate Committee on Foreign Relations, "Putin's Assymetric Assault on Democracy in Russia and Europe: Implications for U.S. National Security," January 10, 2018, https://www.foreign.senate.gov/imo/media/doc/FinalRR.pdf.
10. Center for the Study of Democracy, "Assessing Russia's Economic Footprint in the Western Balkans" (Sofia, 2018), http://www.csd.bg/artShow.php?id=18131.
11. "The Warp of Serbian Identity: Anti-Westernism, Russophilia, Traditionalism," Helsinki Committee for Human Rights in Serbia, Studies no. 17, http://www.helsinki.org.rs/doc/Studies17.pdf.
12. Daniel Serwer and Sinisa Vukovic, "This Is What It Looks Like When Russia Really Wants to Mess with Your Election," *Foreign Policy*, November 8, 2016, https://foreignpolicy.com/2016/11/08/this-is-what-it-looks-like-when-russia-really-wants-to-mess-with-your-election/.
13. "Meeting for Regional Leaders on the Stability Pact, Sarajevo, July 29, 1999," Joint Office for South East Europe, May 1, 2009, http://www.tpk.fi/ahtisaari/puheet-1999/P990729.open.html.
14. "EU–Western Balkans Summit, Thessaloniki, 21 June 2003," European Commission, June 21, 2003, http://europa.eu/rapid/press-release_PRES-03-163_en.htm.
15. Robert Muharremi, "Kosovo Security Force Is an Army: Legal Arguments," Kosovar Centre for Security Studies Policy Brief, March 2016, http://www.qkss.org/en/Policy-Papers/Kosovo-Security-Force-is-an-Army-Legal-Arguments-649.
16. Arolda Elbasani, *European Integration and Transformation in the Western Balkans: Europeanization or Business as Usual?* (New York: Routledge, 2013).
17. Daniel Serwer, "U.S. Policy on the Western Balkans," in *Unfinished Business: The Western Balkans and the International Community*, ed. Vedran Džihić and Daniel Hamilton (Washington, DC: Center for Transatlantic Relations, 2012), 221–29.

18. Susie Alegre, Ivanka Ivanova, and Dana Denis-Smith, *Safeguarding the Rule of Law in an Enlarged EU: The Cases of Bulgaria and Romania*, CEPS Special Report/April 2009 (Center for European Policy Studies, 2009), https://www.ceps.eu/system/files/book/1833.pdf.
19. See, for example, "Lithuania Blocking Chapter Because of Belgrade-Moscow Ties," B92, July 31, 2018, https://www.b92.net/eng/news/politics.php?yyyy=2018&mm=07&dd=31&nav_id=104749.
20. Andrea Lorenzo Capussela, *State-Building in Kosovo: Democracy, Corruption and the EU in the Balkans* (London: I. B. Tauris, 2015).
21. Bobo Weber, "Substantial Change on the Horizon? A Monitoring Report on the EU's New Bosnia and Herzegovina Initiative," Democratization Policy Council, March 2017, http://www.democratizationpolicy.org/pdf/DPC_EU_BiH_Initiative_Monitoring_Report.pdf.
22. "Answers to the Questionnaire," Directorate for European Integration in Bosnia and Herzegovina, http://dei.gov.ba/dei/direkcija/sektor_strategija/Upitnik/odgovoriupitnik/Archive.aspx?pageIndex=1&langTag=en-US.
23. Marco Zambotti, "Questioning Europe's Transformative Power: The EU in Bosnia and Herzegovina, and Kosovo (1995–2015)," (PhD diss., Johns Hopkins University, 2015).
24. Forian Bieber, "Rethinking 'Democratic Backsliding' in Central and Eastern Europe," *East European Politics* 34 (2018): 337–54.
25. Friedrich Ebert Stiftung, "Serbia and Kosovo in 2035: Scenarios," Belgrade, March 2018, http://library.fes.de/pdf-files/bueros/belgrad/14369.pdf.
26. Thomas Risse, Stephen C. Ropp, and Kathryn Sikkink, *The Persistent Power of Human Rights: From Commitment to Compliance* (Cambridge: University Press, 2013).
27. Olga Botcharova, "Implementation of Track Two Diplomacy: Developing a Model of Forgiveness," in *Forgiveness and Reconciliation: Religion, Public Policy, and Conflict Transformation*, ed. Raymond G. Helmick and Rodney L. Petersen (Philadelphia: Templeton Press, 2002), 279–304.
28. Julian Borger, *The Butcher's Trail: How the Search for Balkan War Criminals Became the World's Most Successful Manhunt* (New York: Other Press, 2016).
29. Humanitarian Law Center, "Report on War Crimes Trials in Serbia during 2016," May 2017, http://www.hlc-rdc.org/wp-content/uploads/2017/05/Izvestaj_o_sudjenjima_za_2016_eng.pdf; "Second Report on the Implementation of the National Strategy for the Prosecution of War Crimes," June 2018, http://www.hlc-rdc.org/wp-content/uploads/2018/07/Izvestaj_Strategija_2_ENG-ff.pdf.
30. "RECOM Roadmap Policy Brief," Recom, May 2018, http://recom.link/wp-content/uploads/2018/06/RECOM-Roadmap-ff-1.pdf.

31. Eric Gordy, *Guilt, Responsibility, and Denial: The Past at Stake in Post-Milosevic Serbia* (Philadelphia: University of Pennsylvania Press, 2013).
32. "2017 Corruption Perceptions Index," Transparency International, February 2018, https://www.transparency.org/news/feature/corruption_perceptions_index_2017#table.
33. "Corruption in Kosovo: Bribery as Experienced by the Population," United Nations Office on Drugs and Crime (UNODC), 2011, https://www.unodc.org/documents/data-and-analysis/statistics/corruption/CORRUPTION_KOSOVO_Population.pdf.
34. That is the explicit comparison used in Capussela, *State-Building in Kosovo*.
35. See, for a wealth of detail on Kosovo, Arolda Elbasani, "State-Building or State-Capture? Institutional Exports, Local Reception and Hybridity of Reforms in Post-war Kosovo," *Southeast European and Black Sea Studies* 18, no. 2 (2018): 149–64, https://doi.org/10.1080/14683857.2018.1475901.
36. Arolda Elbasani and Senada Šelo Šabić, "Rule of Law, Corruption and Democratic Accountability in the Course of EU Enlargement," *Journal of European Public Policy* 25, no. 9 (2018): 1317–35, https://doi.org/10.1080/13501763.2017.1315162.
37. Florian Bieber, "The Rise and Fall of Balkan Stabilitocracies," Center for International Relations and Sustainable Development, Winter 2018, https://www.cirsd.org/en/horizons/horizons-winter-2018-issue-no-10/the-rise-and-fall-of-balkan-stabilitocracies.
38. Ivan Krastev, *Shifting Obsessions: Three Essays on the Politics of Anticorruption* (Budapest: Central European University Press, 2004).
39. Human Rights Watch, "The US Global Magnitsky Act: Questions and Answers," September 13, 2017, https://www.hrw.org/news/2017/09/13/us-global-magnitsky-act.
40. Adrian Shtuni, "The Western Balkans," *Fikra Forum*, January 29, 2015. For a comprehensive study and analysis see Anisa Goshi and Dallin Van Leuven, "Kosovo-Wide Assessment of Perceptions of Radicalisation at the Community Level," United Nations Development Programme in Kosovo, May 2017, http://www.ks.undp.org/content/dam/kosovo/docs/PVE/UNDP_KS-Wide%20Assessment_eng_web.pdf.
41. Srecko Latal, "Bosnian Serb Leaders Under Fire Over Loan," Balkan Insight, October 16, 2015, http://www.balkaninsight.com/en/article/new-loan-for-bosnian-serb-entity-triggers-controversy-10-16-2015.
42. Regional Cooperation Council, *South East Europe 2020: Jobs and Prosperity in a European Perspective*, Report, November 2013, https://www.rcc.int/files/user/docs/reports/SEE2020-Strategy.pdf.

Open Access This chapter is distributed under the terms of the Creative Commons Attribution 4.0 International License (http://creativecommons.org/licenses/by/4.0/), which permits use, duplication, adaptation, distribution and reproduction in any medium or format, as long as you give appropriate credit to the original author(s) and the source, a link is provided to the Creative Commons license and any changes made are indicated.

The images or other third party material in this chapter are included in the work's Creative Commons license, unless indicated otherwise in the credit line; if such material is not included in the work's Creative Commons license and the respective action is not permitted by statutory regulation, users will need to obtain permission from the license holder to duplicate, adapt or reproduce the material.

CHAPTER 7

What Should the Middle East and Ukraine Learn from the Balkans?

Abstract The UN-endorsed doctrine known as "Responsibility to Protect" is one important outcome from the Balkans, honored more in the breach than the observance in the Middle East and Ukraine. There are others: leadership is important to starting, preventing, and ending wars; prevention can work, if undertaken early with adequate resources; ethnic partition likely will not; international contributions can be vital; neighborhood counts; power sharing and decentralization can help. Applying these lessons to the Middle East is difficult, not least because there are so many warring parties involved. Ukraine is far simpler and could prove negotiable, but only if Russia, the EU, and the United States are prepared to engage seriously to restore the country's sovereignty while allowing its regions a large measure of autonomy.

Keywords Responsibility to Protect · Leadership · Prevention · Partition · Power sharing · Decentralization

Many people think the Balkan experience bears on other situations, but of course they pick and choose the implications they prefer. Lessons learned are often lessons preferred. Bosnia haunts Syria. Those who favored intervention pointed to the "safe areas" in Bosnia and want something similar in Syria: safe areas, a no-fly zone, or humanitarian corridors. They forget that it was not the safe areas that succeeded in

© The Author(s) 2019
D. Serwer, *From War to Peace in the Balkans, the Middle East and Ukraine*, Palgrave Critical Studies in Post-Conflict Recovery, https://doi.org/10.1007/978-3-030-02173-3_7

Bosnia but rather the NATO bombing that occurred because of the failure of the Serbs to respect the safe areas. Those who want a political settlement in Syria point to the power-sharing arrangement forced on the Bosnians at Dayton. They forget that Dayton entailed major compromises as well as exceedingly slow and difficult implementation. Kosovo is often cited as a precedent for the independence of Kurdistan, which suffered a comparable expulsion of its people, who were gassed as well, but lacks the history of UN administration and the authority of a Security Council resolution promising a final status decision.

Russian President Putin invokes the Balkan example, suggesting that his interest in Crimea and eastern Ukraine derives from humanitarian concern to protect Russian-speakers. He claims to be doing nothing more than what NATO did for Kosovo. Others would suggest that Russia's provision of weapons and support to paramilitaries in Ukraine is a page out of Milošević's playbook, as is his exaggerated complaint about abuse of Russian-speakers and the consequent need for intervention to protect them. Milošević always claimed that he was simply protecting Serbs, even after having fueled with weapons, claims to victimhood, and ethnic hate speech the trouble they found themselves in. Russia is likewise not protecting Russian-speakers but rather generating pretexts for intervention and even, in Crimea, annexation.

The merits and demerits of no-fly zones, safe areas, humanitarian corridors, ethnic division, annexation, self-determination, and the like in Iraq, Syria, or Ukraine have nothing to do with their supposed success, and occasional real failure, in the Balkans. Context matters. 2018 is not 1995. Vladimir Putin's Russia—determined to defy the West, limit NATO expansion, and establish hegemony over Russian-speaking populations in neighboring states—is not Boris Yeltsin's Russia, which was prepared to collaborate with NATO. The United States of Barack Obama and Donald Trump, broke and exhausted after long and costly wars in Afghanistan and Iraq as well as many smaller engagements against agile and protean terrorists—is not the United States of Bill Clinton, riding a giant economic wave and unchallenged militarily worldwide.

The differences are stark. The 1990s were the unipolar moment. Today is the G-zero world.[1] Not only is the unipolar moment over, but nothing has taken its place. The Balkans, geographically and culturally in Europe, is not the Middle East, where authoritarianism survived longer because it was not tied to Communism. Islam in the Balkans is mostly far more moderate than Islam in the Middle East, even if terrorists and their supporters have been discovered in Bosnia and Kosovo and inordinate numbers of foreign fighters have been recruited there.

There are, however, also valid parallels between the Balkans on the one hand and the Middle East and Ukraine on the other. Syria, Iraq, and a large part of North Africa share with most of the Balkans a history in the Ottoman Empire, as does part of southern Ukraine. That is relevant: the Ottomans ruled a multi-sectarian, multi-ethnic empire without homogenizing their populations, the way most European states tried to do, with greater and lesser degrees of success. The *millet* system of the Ottomans allowed different confessional groups to administer their own personal-status laws in distinct courts. Ethnic and sectarian diversity in Syria and Iraq is a legacy of that Ottoman heritage, just as in the Balkans. So too is the second-class treatment of non-"constituent" peoples, that is, those who are not responsible for forming the state. Linguistic diversity in Ukraine is a legacy of the Russian Empire and the Soviet Union, which failed in their efforts to extirpate Ukrainian.

There is another parallel: the Sunni/Shia divide in the Middle East is like the Catholic/Orthodox divide in the Balkans, insofar as it derives originally from a quarrel over who was the proper successor to a recognized leader. While there are today theological, organizational, clerical, and other differences as well, the root of the Sunni/Shia division is the succession to Muhammad. To make a long story short, Shia believe the caliph ("successor") should have been a family relation, specifically, Muhammad's cousin and son-in-law Ali; Sunni disagree and believe that Abu Bakr, a companion of the Prophet, was properly elected as his successor, as well as others who followed (including eventually Ali, who became the fourth caliph). Catholics respect as their religious authority the pope in Rome. Starting in the eleventh century, Orthodox Christians recognized the authority of their own "autocephalous" churches, which are not subordinate to the Roman pope.

But these parallels do not mean any of the approaches taken in 1995 to end the Bosnian War will necessarily work in Ukraine or Syria. A dysfunctional Dayton-style power-sharing arrangement would not be a good outcome in Kiev. There is no reason to believe Bashar al-Assad would allow it in Damascus, now that he appears to be winning Syria's seven-year war. Likewise, what worked for Kosovo would not be workable for the southeastern Ukrainian region of Donbas or for Iraqi Kurdistan, which lacks the internal cohesion required for independence and neighbors prepared to recognize it as a sovereign state.

What might have counted from the Balkans experiences is not Dayton but rather the atrocities and abuses against civilians. "Responsibility to Protect" (R2P) is the UN-endorsed doctrine based on the Balkans and Rwanda tragedies that requires states to protect their populations and allows international intervention under limited circumstances when they do not.[2] R2P cannot help the Syrians or the Ukrainians, because of differences between the United States and Russia in the UN Security Council. But it helped in Libya, where the Security Council authorized a NATO-led intervention in 2011 when Qaddafi threatened to slaughter the population of Benghazi. More recently, the Yezidis of northern Iraq owe their escape from the Sinjar Mountains to American airdrops of humanitarian supplies as well as air strikes against the Islamic State forces, authorized by Baghdad. States today are clearly obligated to protect their civilian populations. If they fail to do so, or cannot, other states can be licensed to intervene in ways that did not exist in Bosnia in 1995. That, more than "Dayton," is a legacy we should respect, but we failed to do so as Aleppo, eastern Ghouta, and southern Syria fell to Russian, Iranian, and Syrian onslaughts. We also failed to do so in Donetsk, Luhansk, and Crimea.

There are some other important lessons worth learning from the Balkans: leadership is important to starting, preventing, and ending wars; prevention can work, if undertaken early with adequate resources; ethnic partition likely will not; international contributions can be vital; neighborhood counts; power sharing and decentralization can help.

LEADERS MATTER

Leaders matter. The Balkan wars would not have happened as they did without Milošević's conversion to Serbian nationalism, based on the claim that Serbs were victims. "All Serbs in one country" promised protection, but it alarmed and excluded non-Serbs, who sought protection on territory they could call their own. Likewise, Iraq's Prime Minister Nouri al-Maliki and Syria's President Bashar al-Assad chose to govern in exclusionary ways that undermined their legitimacy with portions of their countries' populations, triggering sectarian passions and rebellion. Assad, who belongs to the Alawite minority, brutally cracked down on peaceful demonstrations in 2011, driving his opposition to take up arms. Maliki opened Iraq's door to the Islamic State when he tried to repress largely peaceful Sunni demonstrations using force in 2013. One of the first moves by the Ukrainian parliament after pro-Russian President Yanukovych fled was to pass a law denying official status to the Russian language. The law was blocked, but the resentment it generated helped separatists in eastern Ukraine to gain traction with the Donbas region's Russian-speaking population. Inclusion is a key to preserving state integrity. States that rely on mobilizing a part of their population based on identity necessarily exclude others and tend to fail.[3] Inclusion, however, does not necessarily get you elected or keep you in power. Some leaders decide that appealing to only a portion of the population, and repressing the rest, is a better idea. The wars in the Balkans, Syria, Iraq, and Ukraine demonstrate the point.

Leadership matters in the opposition too. When Communism fell, ethnic nationalists in the Balkans were the best organized and equipped to take over. In much of the Middle East, the ideology of political Islam long prevailed among opposition forces.[4] Once the Middle East autocracies began to crumble, Islamists were among the best organized and most united alternatives, not liberal democrats. Those who believe holy scripture is the word of God, and therefore the source of legitimacy and law, have a hard time with government of the people, by the people, and for the people. It should be no surprise that Islamist leadership that insists on sharia law is often intolerant of non-Muslims, non-believers, and liberal democrats. In the most extreme case, the Islamic State insurgency disdained its Shia counterparts, expelled them from territory it controlled, and sought to erase borders in the Middle East. Likewise, Putin and Russophiles in eastern Ukraine would have liked to restore the idea of "Novorossiya," which amounts to a claim that much of Ukraine rightfully belongs to Russia. That would require the expulsion of a lot of Ukrainians and the repression of any who resist. That is not likely in all of Ukraine, but it has already happened in Crimea and to some extent in Donbas. Exclusionary leadership has consequences.

It does not follow, however, that inclusionary ideology has good consequences. Assad's Alawite minority-controlled regime is rhetorically anti-sectarian and tolerant, but it is also autocratic and homicidal. It protects the majority Sunnis and minorities who support the regime, but not the Sunnis and minorities who do not. In more-democratic societies there is at least some chance that leaders will feel pressure to deliver on their ideological commitments. Assad feels none.

Prevention Can Work

Prevention can work, if undertaken early with adequate resources. It did not in Bosnia, because the Europeans and the UN were unwilling and unable to mobilize the resources required. Their deployment of observers first and peacekeepers later was inadequate to make Belgrade and the Bosnian Serbs back down from their effort to create Greater Serbia. Even with American engagement, the same was true in Kosovo.[5] The Macedonian case benefited from an explicitly preventive but still minimalist UN deployment. It worked because Serbia was not prepared to fight for Macedonia and therefore fewer resources were required. One can only wonder what might have been prevented had Syria welcomed an international deployment to help it transition to democracy, rather than chasing the Arab League observers out in 2012. Or if the United States and Europe had been prepared to intervene early to protect civilians. The failure to intervene in August 2013 against Assad for use of chemical weapons is often cited, but the one-off air strikes contemplated then would not have been sufficient to deter Damascus, and it was arguably already too late. Organization for Security and Co-operation in Europe (OSCE) observers in Ukraine are still struggling to monitor cease-fire agreements, as European observers did in Bosnia in the early 1990s, but they are unable to guarantee compliance. Successful prevention requires the willing cooperation of potentially warring parties and international guarantees backed by potential use of force. That is not always available, but when it is it can save lives and prevent disaster.

The top priority in postwar reconstruction efforts is to prevent a return to violence. Dayton implementation after 1995 and the UN protectorate in Kosovo after 1999 thus amounted to largely successful conflict prevention, albeit less formally constituted than in Macedonia. As we have seen in Libya, leaving a war-torn country to its own devices, even if that is what the country's leadership prefers, can lead to catastrophic consequences. But military interventions in Afghanistan and Iraq were unsatisfactory in their outcomes, despite the postwar application of massive military and civilian resources. Conflict prevention through international intervention postwar also works best when it is welcomed, as it was in Bosnia and Kosovo, not resisted, as in Afghanistan and Iraq. Extremist resistance is particularly difficult to handle, since with them a negotiated outcome is often not possible.[6]

The jury is still out in Ukraine. Doubting its capability to pursue two simultaneous wars, Russia toned down the war in the Donbas region in September 2015, to enable its military intervention in Syria. Something like a mutually hurting stalemate may be emerging in Ukraine, with neither the Russian nor the Ukrainian forces seeing much to be gained by continuing the fight. If the "Normandy" powers (France, Germany, Russia, and Ukraine) entrusted with the search for a negotiated solution can find a political way out, or even just freeze the current situation, Ukraine might be able to avoid the kind of wider war that tore Bosnia to shreds and threatened disaster in Kosovo. But it is also still possible that the relative lull in Ukraine will be temporary, presaging an intensified military effort by Moscow and a political effort to prevent Ukraine from tying itself more closely to the EU. The OSCE is walking an unsteady tightrope.

In the Middle East, prevention had its moment in Yemen in late 2011, when the Gulf Cooperation Council managed to get President Ali Abdullah Saleh to leave power in favor of his vice-president, the first step in a multi-phase transition that culminated in a national dialogue in 2013–2014. But the national dialogue failed to resolve key issues concerning the architecture of the state, especially with respect to the northern Houthis as well as the south. With no international force deployed to protect the peace process, a Houthi offensive in 2015 chased the transitional president, whose term had expired, from Sanaa and initiated a civil war that drew in Saudi Arabia and the United Arab Emirates in support of the internationally recognized government as well as Iranian support for the Houthis. Prevention is desirable and relatively cheap, and often worth a try, but it does not always work, especially in the absence of strong international guarantees. Who can provide such guarantees in Yemen once the fighting is over is not clear, making it difficult to negotiate an end to the now internationalized civil war.

Ethnic Partition Likely Will Not Work

A third lesson is about partition, especially redrawing of territorial lines to accommodate ethnic differences. All the current borders of the Balkan states remain where they were in Socialist Yugoslavia. Only their status has been changed, from internal boundaries to international borders. Even in Kosovo, whose population is about 90% Albanian, the international community has so far refused to allow the four northern municipalities, which are contiguous with Serbia and three of which had majority-Serb populations even before the 1999 war, to opt out and rejoin Serbia, despite their relatively recent addition to Kosovo. The Kosovo/Serbia "border"—or for those who do not recognize Kosovo's independence, "boundary"— has not moved.

In the Middle East the international borders are also relatively recent, having been established in the 1920s. They are often attributed to Mark Sykes and François Georges-Picot, British and French diplomats, respectively, but that is not right. Mosul, originally slated for the French colonial mandate under the 1916 Sykes-Picot Agreement and therefore in what we now call Syria, was ceded in 1924 to the British, who already had troops there. The Islamic State, which claimed to be destroying the Sykes-Picot borders, ironically restored them when it absorbed large parts of Iraq's Anbar, Ninewa, and Salaheddin Provinces into a territory they controlled along with eastern Syria. That is how Sykes and Picot had drawn the lines originally.[7]

The borders of Ukraine are even more recent: the Soviet Union transferred Crimea to Kiev's authority only in 1954. Ukraine had emerged as an independent state for the first time, but only briefly, in 1918. It lost part of its territory to Poland and was incorporated into the Soviet Union in 1922.

The question is whether redrawing some of these relatively recent borders to accommodate ethnic or sectarian differences might help to stabilize chronically unstable regions. That is a good question, one ethnic nationalists never tire of asking. The answer is a qualified no. Even if everyone in a region can agree that the borders are arbitrary and should be changed, experience suggests they rarely agree on where they should be redrawn. Czechoslovakia was divided in its 1993 "velvet divorce" peacefully along an agreed preexisting line. In 2011, Sudan was also divided by agreement, but the lines were not so clear. The predictable result was violence focused initially on the Abyei area, where the line was not agreed.

That is the rule. Bosnia's Serbs, Croats, and Bosniaks were unable to agree on their lines of division, which is why they fought. The Vance-Owen plan for drawing ethnic boundaries in Bosnia contributed to the war, not to its solution.[8] Macedonia's ethnic Albanians and ethnic Macedonians know perfectly well that they cannot agree on division of the country. The city with the largest Albanian population in Macedonia is the capital. Any attempt to divide it would mean war. Kosovo's Albanians have until recently insisted on reintegration of the country's

Serbian-majority north not because they are anxious to govern Serbs but because they know partition would call into question their borders with Albania and Macedonia, which Washington and Brussels would not allow. If you open the question of borders in one country, you are bound to cause questioning of borders in other countries in the region and possibly beyond. That is as true of Syria and Iraq in the Middle East as it is of Bosnia and Kosovo in the Balkans.

Iraqi Kurdistan has what many consider a compelling case for independence, which would mean partition of Iraq. Saddam Hussein brutally mistreated the Kurds, chasing them from their homes and even out of the country. He also gassed tens of thousands during the 1986–1989 Anfal campaign. The Kurds have largely governed themselves since 1991, when the United States, Britain, and France imposed a no-fly zone over their territory. Kurdistan won a large measure of autonomy in the 2005 Iraqi constitution, but the relationship between Baghdad and Erbil has been rocky since. The Kurdistan Regional Government (KRG) claims it has not received all the oil revenue it is entitled to, that it has had to defend its own territory from the Islamic State without needed support from Baghdad, and that it faces demands from its population, many of whom no longer speak fluent Arabic, for independence. The KRG claims to be democratic and to treat minorities well. Why should it not be independent?

The geopolitical circumstances are not favorable. While Iraqi Kurdistan has vastly improved its relations with Ankara, large parts of what is now eastern Turkey were slated at the end of World War I to become part of an independent Kurdish state. Turkey does not want to see independence for its southern neighbor while it represses a violent Kurdish rebellion on its own territory, for fear of the irredentist consequences. Iranians feel even more strongly on this issue: fighting frequently flares in Eastern Kurdistan, which is a province of the Islamic Republic. Iran's population is not much more than 60% Persian. Tehran fears the Kurds will not be the only ones looking to get out. Baloch have been rebelling since 2004.

Iraqi Kurds naturally look to the Americans for support. Washington was vital to their survival in the 1990s. The Kurds supported the 2003 U.S. invasion of Iraq and happily hosted American forces. The KRG has welcomed Iraqis of varied sects and ethnicities displaced by ISIS, against whom its Peshmerga fought effectively, and maintains friendly relations with the United States, even welcoming American oil investment and until recently admitting Americans without the visas the

Baghdad government requires. Kurdish friends ask plaintively: Don't the Americans want a friendly ally in the Middle East? One with at least a nominal commitment to multiethnic democracy?

Washington might, but it has global concerns, which include protecting its equities in Baghdad and maintaining the sovereignty and territorial integrity of Georgia, Ukraine, and Moldova, all of which have Russian-supported territories wanting to secede. Independence for Kurdistan would open the proverbial Pandora's box, strengthening Putin's arguments and undermining the international consensus that has formed against independence for South Ossetia and Abkhazia, the annexation of Crimea, and the rebellion in Donetsk and Luhansk, as well as the aspirations of Moldova's Transnistria. China is no less opposed to Kurdistan independence than the Americans, for fear of the implications for Tibet. Geopolitics are not sympathetic to Kurdish aspirations.

Inside Iraq, there are other issues. Kurdistan's main political parties all agree on independence as their goal, but none are willing to see the others get credit for it. Former Kurdistan Regional President Mustafa Barzani locked his opposition out of parliament and was none too gentle with those in the press and civil society who tried to buck his authority. The boundaries of Iraqi Kurdistan are not agreed. While the KRG seized the so-called disputed territories during its offensive against the Islamic State in 2014, Baghdad did not agree that they belong within Kurdistan. The KRG offered to conduct referenda in these territories on whether they would want to join with Kurdistan, fulfilling a provision of the Iraqi constitution. But doing that in the absence of international supervision and with the KRG in control was not going to convince Baghdad that a free choice had been made.

At oil prices around $50 per barrel in 2017, the KRG was nowhere near having the financial resources to be independent. Independence would have left Kurdistan even worse off. It is an oil rentier state, despite its hopes for a more diversified economy. Oil prices in the future will have a hard time going over $80 per barrel for a sustained period, because above that level massive quantities of unconventionally produced oil and gas (as well as other alternatives) will come online. The KRG needs closer to $100 per barrel to meet its financial requirements with oil production well above current levels.

Barzani nevertheless proceeded with an independence referendum in September 2017, which predictably won approval by a wide margin. He claimed it would be prelude to renegotiation of the relationship with

Baghdad, not necessarily a one-way street to independence. Anyone who knows Kurds would doubt that after voting independence they would return to the negotiating table to accept some sort of confederal arrangement to stay nominally inside Iraq. An independence referendum was far more likely to trigger still another violent conflict, in which Arabs (both Sunni and Shia) would fight Kurds to determine the borders they had failed to agree on for more than a decade.

That is what happened, though on a relatively small scale. Iraqi Prime Minister Haider al-Abadi, fresh from victory over the Islamic State, used his battle-hardened forces to retake most of the disputed territories, with some mostly passive help from Barzani's political rivals. The redrawing of sovereign borders in the Middle East suffered a resounding setback.

Partition has also been proposed for Syria. Henri Barkey, a distinguished scholar of the Middle East, proposed ethnic/sectarian division of the country into three parts: Alawite and Christian in the west, Kurdish in the north, and Sunni in the center.[9] The trouble is that the population is not distributed that way. The Alawites have never been a majority in the main population centers of the west, to which many Sunnis have fled because of the war. Kurdish populations in the north are mixed with Arabs. Christians and other minorities are embedded among the Sunnis. Many Alawites live in Damascus. Drawing ethnic and sectarian lines would lead to a bloodbath in Syria as each group seeks to establish a majority in its designated area.

Crimea represents a possible exception to the rule. Its border is not in doubt, and its transfer to Ukraine was recent. President Trump has indicated some sympathy for the Russian annexation of a territory where most people speak Russian. Much of Crimea's population, though not the minority Tatars, appeared to welcome the peninsula's transfer back to Russian rule, though only time will tell whether that attitude is permanent. The March 2014 referendum was not free or fair. Conducted under Russian military occupation, it failed to offer an option to remain with Crimea's relatively autonomous status within Ukraine. Tens of thousands of Crimean Tatars and Ukrainians have been chased from their homes. Both the UN General Assembly and Security Council overwhelmingly voted their disapproval, but General Assembly resolutions are not binding.[10] Russia vetoed Security Council action, claiming that Kosovo set a precedent for what was done with Crimea.

The analogy is false. Crimea had no UN peacekeeping forces or UN administration. It was seized by force, not occupied in accordance with a

Security Council resolution. Only a handful of countries have recognized its annexation. It is costing Moscow a bundle. The Americans and Europeans are refusing to accept the annexation, as they did with the Baltic states when incorporated into the Soviet Union at the end of World War II.[11] They hope some future Russian government will implement a negotiated settlement for Crimea, one that returns it to Ukrainian sovereignty but with a great deal of autonomy. The Russians hope for the inverse: American recognition of the annexation of Crimea (and perhaps also the "independence" of South Ossetia and Abkhazia) in exchange for Russian acceptance of Kosovo's independence.

In the Middle East, Pandora's box now contains oil and gas, which intensifies conflicts over territory. The Iraqi city of Kirkuk has long been disputed among Kurds, Arabs, and Turkmen. Its oil and gas production raises the stakes. The Syrian government wants to regain control of the country's eastern oil and gas fields, now in the hands of the Syrian Democratic Forces whom the Americans backed in the battles against the Islamic State in eastern Syria. Fuel and hydrocarbon revenue could be critical in the postwar period. Likewise, Iraq's Sunnis are not going to allow Iraq's south to walk off with the country's massive reserves. Partition of Iraq or Syria is a bad idea because it would cause more war, not end it. In the Middle East and Ukraine as much as in the Balkans, attempts at ethnoterritorial partition are bound to generate atrocities and other human rights abuses.

Neighborhood Counts

Neighborhood is a key factor in determining the outcome of war.[12] The Balkans lies between Greece and the rest of the EU. It is not surprising that the region eventually found a better trajectory than the one it traced in the 1990s, even if it is now struggling to maintain its European ambitions. Though historians and geographers are fond of the Mediterranean basin as a unifying theme for the countries of its littoral, Europe and the Middle East have not been on the same wavelength for a millennium. European efforts to promote trade and investment with the Middle East and to export liberal values have failed.[13] Only Turkey among Middle Eastern countries once enjoyed the theoretical prospect of eventual EU membership, but President Erdoğan's autocratic impulses are now all too obvious. The Middle East is a decidedly bad neighborhood if you are looking for models of good governance and rule of law.

Iraqi Kurdistan is a possible exception. It has pretensions to Western values, but its duopoly has been less than liberal when it comes to freedom of expression, and its courts fall far short of independence. Kurdistan has had to worry more about security issues than reform. It is also plagued with the endemic corruption associated with oil revenues, whose disposition has been far from transparent. If your nearest neighbors are Iran, Arab Iraq, Syria, and southeastern Turkey (where repression of Kurds has been strong for decades), liberal democracy is not the first governance system that comes to mind.

Ukraine counts EU members Romania and Poland among its neighbors, in addition to Russia and Belarus. The predictable result is ambiguity. While many Ukrainians in the western part of the country prefer to follow a European model, the east is closely tied to Russia. Kiev, which counts Brussels among its key supporters and seeks eventual EU membership, has been slow to institute reforms, but the pressure is strong. Ukraine is fortunate to have the Brussels pole exerting its attractive force.

The Middle East lacks this teleological drive. There is no magnet pulling the countries of the failed 2011 Arab uprisings (Egypt, Yemen, Syria, and Libya) in a more democratic direction or offering a state paradigm based on rule of secular law. The only model of moderate political reform in the Arab Middle East is Tunisia, which is too small, too far removed from the Middle East's center of gravity, and too close to the starting gate to pull others in its barely perceptible wake. There are more models that point in the monarchical and autocratic directions. The kings of Jordan and Morocco have instituted modest reforms, but they remain illiberal, even if nominally constitutional at best. The Gulf monarchies, especially Saudi Arabia, the United Arab Emirates, and Bahrain, are more inclined to autocracy, even when pursuing reforms. Saudi Arabia and the UAE have also been willing to use their deep pockets of oil revenue to sponsor secular autocrats in other countries, especially Egypt and Jordan, while Qatar has used its vast natural gas revenue to fund the Muslim Brotherhood and other Islamists.

The lack of a nearby, attractive, pluralistic, democratic model, current or historical, is profoundly important.[14] While Muslims in Indonesia and elsewhere have come to enjoy democracy, in the Middle East its roots are shallow. Association with military autocracy has tainted secularism. The courts that administer law in secular Middle Eastern autocracies have been loyal tools of repression. The result is wide and apparently growing appeal of sharia, Islamic jurisprudence. The Islamic State's brutal caliphate has far more resonance in the Middle East than liberal democracy.

The Middle East needs a set of norms, like those the OSCE promulgated starting with the 1975 Helsinki Final Act, which set out agreed principles and attempt to channel competition into peaceful rivalry, reducing the incentive states feel to repress minorities, even when the states are autocratic.[15] If Iran and Saudi Arabia feared each other less, they would do less to repress the minority Sunni and Shia who inhabit their respective territories, as well as those of their neighbors. If they had an organization like the OSCE, or even the less norm-based Association of Southeast Asian Nations, managing the conflicts that do arise would be far more likely to keep the peace. Peaceful coexistence as a regional goal is a low bar, but it would represent a distinct improvement over the current situation.[16]

International Contributions Can Be Vital

Eventually, foreign military intervention ended the slaughter in the Balkans. It worked in Libya when Qaddafi threatened mass atrocities in Benghazi. Libya's deterioration from late 2012 onward should not hide the success of the NATO-led air campaign.[17] American airpower was vital in helping Iraqi as well as Syrian Kurdish-led forces turn the tide against the Islamic State and its atrocities from 2015 onward.

The United States hesitated, however, to intervene against Assad in Syria. The CNN effect has faded, because of the wide availability of atrocity photographs and videos. We are inured. Tired of being the world's policeman, Washington refused even to act as its fireman, putting out a conflagration that caused massive refugee flows to Turkey, Lebanon, Jordan, and even Europe. Russia has been bolder: it massed troops on Ukraine's border to slow Kiev's advance into Donbas, then invaded southeastern Ukraine in late 2014 to protect the separatists when Kiev ignored the threat. In 2015, Russia established an air base in Syria, from which it has bombed mainly moderate opposition forces to prop up President Assad. This is ironic: a Russia that portrays itself as a principled advocate of national sovereignty opposed to anti-constitutional intervention in Syria is breaching both sovereignty and constitutionality in Ukraine, not many kilometers away.

Foreign intervention does not always mean military force. Economic and financial sanctions are far more common. They rarely work quickly when imposed. But relief from sanctions as part of negotiated political settlement can be a powerful diplomatic tool. Milošević negotiated long and hard for relief from sanctions, which were suspended in return for his adherence to the Dayton agreements. Putin has used the imposition of sanctions to rally Russians against the West. But he will no doubt someday be looking for relief from them in any settlement of the Ukraine conflict. Draconian UN sanctions on Iran brought Tehran to the bargaining table, but it was only relief from them that enabled the now-abandoned nuclear deal to be concluded. Relief from sanctions will no doubt be important in the negotiation of any political settlements in Syria as well as Yemen.

International contributions are not limited to military force and sanctions, which are blunt instruments. Diplomacy matters. It is far easier between two parties than among three or more. War in Bosnia was three-sided: the Croat Defense Council fought the Bosnian Army in 1992 and 1993 even as both fought together against the Bosnian Serb Army. The United States provided vital support to the UN in ending the fighting between the Croats and the Bosnian Army, thus reducing a three-party problem to a far easier, if still complex, two-party conflict at Dayton. In Iraq the fight against the Islamic State was mainly a two-party conflict, with Iraqi Kurdistan, Baghdad's various forces (including Iranian-supported militias), and the Americans in coalition against the Islamic State. Ukraine is mainly a two-party conflict, between Kiev and secessionists in the Donbas.

In Syria it is hard even to count the number of different parties involved: the government and its allied militias, Iran and its allied militias, Russia and its allied militias, Turkey and its allied militias, the Israelis, the Americans and allied European forces, as well as Arab, Kurdish, and secular militias, non-jihadi Islamist forces, the Islamic State, and Al Qaeda. The geometry of the relationships among them is not only complex; it is also variable. While the Russians have had some success in negotiating de-escalation zones that lead to surrenders, simplification of the equation is needed before negotiating a country-wide solution.

International guarantees of peace implementation are a particularly important factor in negotiating an end to war.[18] The Americans and Europeans made it clear at Dayton that they would ensure implementation of any agreement reached there. The UN, supported by a NATO-led force, was committed, with Security Council support, to implementation of Resolution 1244, which ended the Kosovo War.

In Ukraine there is some hope that UN peacekeepers might be deployed in the east to guarantee a peace agreement, if one is reached. But who could provide guarantees in Syria? At this point it is only the Russians and Iranians who would be willing, and they are committed to keeping Assad in power. The peace he imposes will seek to ensure his own security and hold on a "fierce" state, with the goal of restoring autocratic political and economic control.[19]

How a war ends obviously affects what happens thereafter, but not only in the expected ways. A flawed Dayton agreement froze the conflict in Bosnia and made it a less than fully functional state but still allowed Croatia to move in a more European direction. An equally flawed UN Security Council resolution ended the Kosovo war with ambiguity about its status but nevertheless enabled Serbia to begin to shed Milošević's autocracy and move toward Europe. Assad's fierce state may prove less resilient than he would like and less able to control parts of the country. The failure of the United States to end the wars in Afghanistan and Iraq with a definitive document marking the end of hostilities left the door open to continued insurgencies. It was a mistake not to insist that some Taliban commander or Iraqi army general sit at a table and sign on the dotted line. This is far more important for postwar developments than the more noted failure to declare war.[20]

Power Sharing and Decentralization Can Help

The Balkan wars of the 1990s, like the Arab uprisings of 2011 and the insurgency in Ukraine, were struggles over power and how it should be distributed. Power sharing at the national level has been an important part of the solution throughout the Balkans. Bosnia has rigid constitutional arrangements, imposed at Dayton, that require power sharing and make the country difficult to govern. Others have come to it more organically and less rigidly, but it now exists in one form or another throughout much of former Yugoslavia. Also important has been decentralization, which allows minorities to govern in local areas where they are in the majority. Municipal and provincial councils provide opportunities to share power that would be difficult to realize at the national level. They also provide opportunities for patronage that can be useful in pacifying minorities. The Minsk II agreement for Ukraine, if ever implemented, will provide ample opportunities for decentralized governance in the rebellious parts of Ukraine.

In the Middle East, only Iraq, Tunisia, and Morocco have really tried serious power sharing at the national level. It worked, with hiccups, in Tunisia during the transition to a new constitution. It is working in Morocco as well, though the king remains in charge while sharing power over non-security issues with an Islamist-led government. In Iraq, power sharing among Shia, Sunni, and Kurds has been less successful. Their squabbling paralyzed Iraq during much of the prime ministry of Nouri al-Maliki, but it is hard to see how Iraq could be governed today without power sharing.

What has worked better in Iraq than national-level power sharing is decentralization. Power devolved to the KRG and to the Shia provinces has enabled those areas to continue reasonably stable governance even as the Islamic State took over the Sunni west and north. Decentralized democracy is a messy system but can be far less fragile than centralized autocracy, which depends for its survival on a Bashar al-Assad, Saddam Hussein, or Muammar Qaddafi. If Libya is to survive as a single state, it will need to devolve power to its regions and municipalities, which even today continue to function despite the national and regional instability. The same is true of troubled Yemen. Neither the Houthis nor South Yemen is likely to return to rule from Sanaa. Inclusion and empowerment, so important to stable governance, begin at the local level, where it is often harder to define issues in purely sectarian or ethnic terms. Filling the potholes and providing water are service issues, not identity ones.

Conclusion

More than twenty-three years will have passed since Dayton when you read this book. Rarely during those years were people in the Balkans optimistic about the future. The major Balkan protagonists—Bosniaks, Croats, Serbs, Albanians, and Macedonians—all feel unsatisfied. They complain that their states are corrupt and dysfunctional, their adversaries unjustly rewarded, their international friends insufficiently supportive. The same is true in the Middle East and Ukraine. Pessimism is rife. Since the outbreak of the Arab uprisings in early 2011 things seem only to have gotten more complicated and difficult. In Ukraine, Russia continues its occupation of Crimea and parts of the southeast.

The election of Donald Trump casts a long shadow on the Balkans, the Middle East, and Ukraine. The president admires Putin's leadership style, likes most autocrats, and sympathizes with ethnic nationalism both at home and abroad. His former campaign aides are busily marketing their services to Balkan ethno-nationalists.[21] American support for liberal democracy, free trade, and open investment has weakened. Some think Trump aims to destroy the West.[22] The president disdains international norms and views the world as disordered, hostile, and chaotic. That is a self-fulfilling prophecy, since the United States has been one of the key forces in sustaining the post-World War II international order. Ignoring this vital role, Trump puts his understanding of American interests first. He shows little interest in American ideals.

This attitude could have dramatic repercussions not only in the Balkans but also in Ukraine and the Middle East. Would-be autocrats in both regions are enjoying reduced pressures for democracy, rule of law, human rights, and open economies. While the State Department has pronounced the United States opposed to the Russian annexation of Crimea, it will not be surprising if the president still leans toward ethnic division in Ukraine. The administration opposed Iraqi Kurdistan's independence, but so late in the game that the referendum could not be blocked. Even serious consideration of partition anywhere in the Balkans, the Middle East, or Ukraine could trigger partition pushes elsewhere. Kosovo, Macedonia, Bosnia, and even Serbia could see ethnoterritorial ambitions reignited in ways that would be difficult to contain. Kurdish aspirations could put Turkey and Iran at risk. Iraq, Syria, Yemen, and Libya would also find the centrifugal forces their civil wars have already unleashed strengthened.

What the Balkans, the Middle East, and Ukraine need are principled commitments by their own politicians to move in the democratic and free-market direction. This unity of purpose will require eschewing ethno-sectarian appeals and partition, looking for ways to share power and decentralize to make governance more inclusive, blocking theft of state assets as well as other forms of corruption, seeking international assistance and guarantees to prevent conflict, and searching for models and helpful neighbors wherever they may be found. These are not difficult remedies, but they require thoughtful leadership, assiduous pursuit, and long-term perspectives.

Clarity about objectives is particularly important. If you know the right direction and keep moving, however slowly, you make progress. That is the best news from the Balkans. It would also be good news for Ukraine and the Middle East, if ever they can find a compass and begin the long, slow slog to more democratic, prosperous, and secure outcomes.

Notes

1. Ian Bremmer, *Every Nation for Itself: Winners and Losers in a G-Zero World* (London: Portfolio, 2013).
2. United Nations Office on Genocide Prevention and the Responsibility to Protect, "Responsibility to Protect," http://www.un.org/en/genocide-prevention/about-responsibility-to-protect.html.
3. Inclusion is the common theme of Daron Acemoglu and James A. Robinson, *Why Nations Fail: The Origins of Power, Prosperity, and Poverty* (New York: Crown, 2012); World Bank Group and United Nations, *Pathways for Peace: Inclusive Approaches for Preventing Violent Conflict* (Washington, DC: World Bank, 2018), https://openknowledge.worldbank.org/handle/10986/28337; Charles Call, *Why Peace Fails: The Causes and Prevention of Civil War Recurrence* (Washington, DC: Georgetown University Press, 2012); and Andreas Wimmer, *Nation Building: Why Some Countries Come Together While Others Fall Apart* (Princeton: Princeton University Press, 2018).
4. Shadi Hamid, *Temptations of Power: Islamists and Illiberal Democracy in a New Middle East* (New York: Oxford University Press, 2014).
5. For the multiple prevention failures in former Yugoslavia, see I. William Zartman, *Cowardly Lions: Missed Opportunities to Prevent Deadly Conflict and State Collapse* (Boulder, CO: Lynne Rienner, 2005), 137–80.
6. Barbara F. Walter, "The New New Civil Wars," *Annual Review of Political Science*, no. 20 (2017): 469–86.
7. Sara Pursley, "'Lines Drawn on an Empty Map': Iraq's Borders and the Legend of the Artificial State (Part 1)," *Jadaliyya*, June 2, 2015, http://www.jadaliyya.com/Details/32140/%60Lines-Drawn-on-an-Empty-Map%60-Iraq's-Borders-and-the-Legend-of-the-Artificial-State-Part-1.
8. Matjaž Klemenčič, "The International Community and the FRY/Belligerents, 1989–1997," in *Confronting the Yugoslav Controversies: A Scholars' Initiative*, ed. Charles W. Ingrao and Thomas A. Emmert (West Lafayette, IN: Purdue University Press, 2009), 153–98.
9. Henri J. Barkey, "A U.S. Blueprint for Syria," *The American Interest*, January 27, 2016, https://www.the-american-interest.com/2016/01/27/a-u-s-blueprint-for-syria/.
10. "Resolution Adopted by the General Assembly on 27 March 2014," https://undocs.org/A/RES/68/262.
11. This position has been formalized by the State Department (not, however, by the White House); see Secretary of State Michael R. Pompeo, "Crimea Statement," July 25, 2018, https://www.state.gov/secretary/remarks/2018/07/284508.htm.
12. Christoph Zürcher, Carrie Manning, Kristie D. Evenson, Rachel Hayman, Sarah Riese, and Nora Roehner, "Neighborhood," in *Costly Democracy:*

Peacebuilding and Democratization after War (Stanford: Stanford University Press, 2013), 112–30.
13. Aylin Ünver Noi, *The Euro-Mediterranean Partnership and the Broader Middle East and North Africa Initiative: Competing or Complementary Projects?* (Lanham, MD: University Press of America, 2011).
14. "The Tragedy of the Arabs," *Economist*, July 5, 2014, https://www.economist.com/leaders/2014/07/05/the-tragedy-of-the-arabs.
15. Caveat emptor: I am affiliated with a Middle East Dialogue that aims to develop such a set of principles; see "The Baghdad Declaration: Good Neighborhood Principles for the Middle East," Middle East Institute, February 2018, http://www.mei.edu/content/baghdad-declaration-good-neighborhood-principles-middle-east. Notably, the first principle includes territorial integrity of the existing states.
16. Paul Salem, "The Road Less Traveled: Potential Pathways from Disorder to Order in the Middle East," in *From Chaos to Cooperation: Toward Regional Order in the Middle East*, ed. Ross Harrison and Paul Salem (Washington, DC: Middle East Institute, 2017), 1–14.
17. Frederic Wehrey, *The Burning Shores: Inside the Battle for the New Libya* (New York: Farrar, Straus and Giroux, 2018).
18. Barbara F. Walter, *Committing to Peace: The Successful Settlement of Civil Wars* (Princeton: Princeton University Press, 2002).
19. Steven Heydemann, "Beyond Fragility: Syria and the Challenges of Reconstruction in Fierce States," Brookings, June 2018, https://www.brookings.edu/wp-content/uploads/2018/06/FP_20180626_beyond_fragility.pdf.
20. Tanisha M. Fazal, "Why States No Longer Declare War," *Security Studies* 21, no. 4 (2012): 557–93, https://www.tandfonline.com/doi/abs/10.1080/09636412.2012.734227.
21. Casey Michel, "Ex-Trump Campaign Officials Are Now Appearing with Pro-Moscow Separatist Leaders," ThinkProgress, June 15, 2018, https://thinkprogress.org/these-trump-campaign-officials-are-causing-trouble-in-bosnia-2873f3e205c4/.
22. David Leonhardt, "Trump Tries to Destroy the West," *New York Times*, June 10, 2018, https://www.nytimes.com/2018/06/10/opinion/g7-trump-quebec-trudeau.html.

Open Access This chapter is distributed under the terms of the Creative Commons Attribution 4.0 International License (http://creativecommons.org/licenses/by/4.0/), which permits use, duplication, adaptation, distribution and reproduction in any medium or format, as long as you give appropriate credit to the original author(s) and the source, a link is provided to the Creative Commons license and any changes made are indicated.

The images or other third party material in this chapter are included in the work's Creative Commons license, unless indicated otherwise in the credit line; if such material is not included in the work's Creative Commons license and the respective action is not permitted by statutory regulation, users will need to obtain permission from the license holder to duplicate, adapt or reproduce the material.

Selected Bibliography

Acemoglu, Daron, and James A. Robinson. *Why Nations Fail: The Origins of Power, Prosperity, and Poverty.* New York: Crown, 2012.

Bieber, Florian. *Post-war Bosnia: Ethnicity, Inequality and Public Sector Governance.* Houndmills, Basingstoke, Hampshire: Palgrave Macmillan, 2006.

———. "The Rise (and Fall) of Balkan Stabilitocracies." *Horizons*, no. 10 (Winter 2018): 176–85. https://www.cirsd.org/en/horizons/horizons-winter-2018-issue-no-10/the-rise-and-fall-of-balkan-stabilitocracies.

———. "Rethinking 'Democratic Backsliding' in Central and Eastern Europe." *East European Politics* 34 (2018): 337–54.

Borger, Julian. *The Butcher's Trail: How the Search for Balkan War Criminals Became the World's Most Successful Manhunt.* New York: Other Press, 2016.

Bosch, E., et al. "Paternal and Maternal Lineages in the Balkans Show a Homogeneous Landscape Over Linguistic Barriers, Except for the Isolated Aromuns." *Annals of Human Genetics* 70, no. 4 (July 2006): 459–87. http://www.carswell.com.au/wp-content/documents/homogenous-balkan-analysis.pdf.

Burg, Steven L., and Paul S. Shoup. *The War in Bosnia-Herzegovina: Ethnic Conflict and International Intervention.* Armonk, NY: M. E. Sharpe, 1999.

Call, Charles. *Why Peace Fails: The Causes and Prevention of Civil War Recurrence.* Washington, DC: Georgetown University Press, 2012.

Caplan, Richard. *Europe and the Recognition of New States in Yugoslavia.* Cambridge: Cambridge University Press, 2005.

Center for the Study of Democracy. "Assessing Russia's Economic Footprint in the Western Balkans: Corruption and State Capture Risks." Sofia: Center for the Study of Democracy, 2018. http://www.csd.bg/artShow.php?id=18131.

Chollet, Derek. *The Road to the Dayton Accords: A Study of American Statecraft.* New York: Palgrave Macmillan, 2005.

Dobbins, James, Laurel E. Miller, Stephanie Pezard, Christopher S. Chivvis, Julie E. Taylor, Keith Crane, Calin Trenkov-Wermuth, and Tewodaj Mengistu. *Overcoming Obstacles to Peace: Local Factors in Nation-Building.* Santa Monica, CA: RAND, 2013. https://www.rand.org/pubs/research_reports/RR167.html. Also available in print form.

Elbasani, Arolda. *European Integration and Transformation in the Western Balkans: Europeanization or Business as Usual?* New York: Routledge, 2013.

———. "State-Building or State-Capture? Institutional Exports, Local Reception and Hybridity of Reforms in Post-war Kosovo." *Southeast European and Black Sea Studies* (2018). https://doi.org/10.1080/14683857.2018.1475901.

Gordy, Eric. *Guilt, Responsibility, and Denial: The Past at Stake in Post-Milosevic Serbia.* Philadelphia: University of Pennsylvania Press, 2013.

Hamid, Shadi. *Temptations of Power: Islamists and Illiberal Democracy in a New Middle East.* New York: Oxford University Press, 2014.

Harrison, Ross, and Paul Salem, eds. *From Chaos to Cooperation: Toward Regional Order in the Middle East.* Washington, DC: Middle East Institute, 2017.

Hays, Don, and Jason Crosby. "From Dayton to Brussels: Constitutional Preparations for Bosnia's EU Accession." Washington, DC: United States Institute of Peace, 2006. https://www.usip.org/publications/2006/10/dayton-brussels-constitutional-preparations-bosnias-eu-accession.

Heydemann, Steven. "Beyond Fragility: Syria and the Challenges of Reconstruction in Fierce States." June 2018. https://www.brookings.edu/wp-content/uploads/2018/06/FP_20180626_beyond_fragility.pdf.

Hockenos, Paul. *Homeland Calling: Exile Patriotism and the Balkan Wars.* Ithaca: Cornell University Press, 2003.

Holbrooke, Richard C. *To End a War.* New York: Random House, 1998.

Ingrao, Charles W., and Thomas Allan Emmert, eds. *Confronting the Yugoslav Controversies: A Scholars' Initiative.* West Lafayette, IN: Purdue University Press, 2009.

Janjić, Dušan. "Normalization Challenges: Analysis of the Negotiation Process and the Implementation of the Brussels Agreement." Belgrade: Forum for Ethnic Relations Policy Paper, 2015.

Ker-Lindsay, James. *Kosovo: The Path to Contested Statehood in the Balkans.* London: I. B. Tauris, 2009.

Knaus, Gerald, and Felix Martin, "Lessons from Bosnia and Herzegovina: Travails of the European Raj." *Journal of Democracy* 14, no. 3 (July 2003): 60–74. https://www.journalofdemocracy.org/article/lessons-bosnia-and-herzegovina-travails-european-raj.

Krastev, Ivan. *Shifting Obsessions: Three Essays on the Politics of Anticorruption.* New York: Central European University Press, 2004.

Lund, Michael S., "Preventive Diplomacy for Macedonia, 1992–1999: From Containment to Nation Building." In *Opportunities Missed, Opportunities Seized: Preventive Diplomacy in the Post-Cold War World*, edited by Bruce W. Jentleson. Lanham, MD: Rowman & Littlefield, 2000.

Mertus, Julie. *Kosovo: How Myths and Truths Started a War.* Berkeley: University of California Press, 1999.

Mujanovic, Jasmin. *Hunger and Fury: The Crisis of Democracy in the Balkans.* Oxford: Oxford University Press, 2018.

Regan, Patrick. *Civil Wars and Foreign Powers: Outside Intervention in Intrastate Conflict.* Ann Arbor: University of Michigan Press, 2000.

Regional Cooperation Council. *South East Europe 2020: Jobs and Prosperity in a European Perspective.* November 2013.

Sell, Louis. *Slobodan Milošević and the Destruction of Yugoslavia.* Durham: Duke University Press, 2002.

Sells, Michael Anthony. *The Bridge Betrayed: Religion and Genocide in Bosnia.* Berkeley: University of California Press, 1996.

United Nations Office on Genocide Prevention and the Responsibility to Protect. "Responsibility to Protect." http://www.un.org/en/genocideprevention/about-responsibility-to-protect.html.

United States Senate Committee on Foreign Relations. "Putin's Asymmetric Assault on Democracy in Russia and Europe: Implications for U.S. National Security." January 10, 2018. https://www.foreign.senate.gov/imo/media/doc/FinalRR.pdf.

Walter, Barbara F. *Committing to Peace: The Successful Settlement of Civil Wars.* Princeton: Princeton University Press, 2002.

———. "The New New Civil Wars." *Annual Review of Political Science* 20, no. 1 (2017): 469–86.

Wehrey, Frederic. *The Burning Shores: Inside the Battle for the New Libya.* New York: Farrar, Straus and Giroux, 2018.

Williams, Abiodun. *Preventing War: The United Nations and Macedonia.* Lanham, MD: Rowman & Littlefield, 2000.

Wimmer, Andreas. *Nation Building: Why Some Countries Come Together While Others Fall Apart.* Princeton: Princeton University Press, 2018.

Woodward, Susan L. *Balkan Tragedy: Chaos and Dissolution After the Cold War.* Washington, DC: Brookings Institution, 1997.

World Bank Group and United Nations. *Pathways for Peace: Inclusive Approaches for Preventing Violent Conflict.* Washington, DC: The World Bank, 2018. https://openknowledge.worldbank.org/handle/10986/28337.

Zambotti, Marco. "Questioning Europe's Transformative Power: The EU in Bosnia and Herzegovina, and Kosovo (1995–2015)." PhD diss., Johns Hopkins University, 2015.

Index

A
Abdel Fattah el-Sisi, 23
Abkhazia, 47, 86, 124, 126
Afghanistan, 1, 14, 22, 62–64, 116, 120, 130
Ahmeti, Ali, 67
Ahtisaari, Martti, 81, 82, 89
Ahtisaari Plan, 82–84
Albania, 3, 10, 22, 54, 55, 57–59, 67, 73, 74, 82, 83, 92, 96, 99, 103, 105, 108, 123
Albanian question, 20, 58, 62, 82
Albanian rebellion, 16, 58, 59, 73
Ali Abdullah Saleh, 121
Ali Ahmeti, 59
Al Qaeda, 13, 129
April package, 41–43, 46
Arbitration, 12, 40
Arkan (Ražnatović, Željko), 74

B
Badinter Commission, 7, 31
Baker, James, 15, 31
Barzani, Mustafa, 124
Bashar al-Assad, 117–120, 128, 130, 131
Battle of Kosovo Polje, 19
Berlin Wall, 4, 15, 29, 30, 93, 104, 107, 108
Bildt, Carl, 39
Bonn powers, 40, 42, 79
Bosnia, 1–3, 5–11, 13, 14, 16–18, 20–22, 24, 26, 29, 31–36, 38–51, 53, 55, 59, 64, 71, 73–75, 77–80, 82, 84, 86, 91, 94–98, 100–103, 105, 107–109, 111, 115–118, 120–123, 129, 130, 132
Bosniaks, 7, 9, 10, 20, 31–34, 36, 39, 44, 46, 54, 78, 86, 102, 122, 131
Bosnian Serb Army (VRS), 17, 34, 35, 37, 129
Brexit, 3, 13, 85, 93
Brussels agreement, 83–85, 89, 99
Bulgaria, 10, 54, 92, 93, 99, 103, 111
Bush, George H.W., 17

C

CeSID (the Center for Free Elections and Democracy), 76, 77
Chetniks, 9
Chirac, Jacques (French President Chirac), 17
Christopher, Warren, 17
Clinton, Bill, 17, 18, 55, 116
CNN effect, 16, 128
Cold War, 4, 5, 11, 13, 15, 17, 18, 24–26, 99
Communism, 9, 15, 68, 76, 78, 116, 119
Council of Europe, 41, 95
Council on Foreign Relations, 14, 24, 110
Crimea, 21, 31, 47, 86, 96, 116, 118, 119, 122, 124–126, 131, 132
Croat Defence Force (HVO), 34, 36
Croatia, 3, 5, 7–9, 11, 14, 16, 20–22, 29–31, 33–35, 40, 44, 46–48, 54, 55, 64, 72–74, 77, 78, 92, 93, 96–98, 102, 103, 108, 109, 130
Cyprus, 101

D

Dayton, 1, 4, 6, 14, 18, 32, 34–41, 43–46, 48–50, 65, 73, 74, 76, 80, 91, 116–118, 120, 129–131
Decentralization, 45, 53, 58, 60, 115, 118, 130, 131
Democratic League of Kosovo (LDK), 80
Democratic Union for Integration (DUI), 59
Đinđić, Zoran, 77, 78, 88
Dimitrov, Nikola, 65
Dodik, Milorad, 42, 43, 45, 97
Dole, Robert, 17
Donbas, 117, 119, 121, 128, 129
Draskovic, Vuk, 77
Drenica massacre, 73
Đukanović, Milo, 20, 95, 105

E

Egypt, 23, 127
Eide, Kai, 81, 84
Erdoğan, Recep Tayyip, 44, 126
Erdut Agreement, 5
EULEX, 82–84
European Court of Human Rights, 42
European Union (EU), 2, 3, 6, 10, 14, 17, 18, 22, 23, 31, 32, 41–47, 50, 53, 60–66, 71, 78, 79, 81–85, 91–109, 115, 121, 126, 127
Extremists, 13, 21, 33, 36

F

Ferdinand, Franz (Austrian archduke), 18
Financial crisis, 22, 40, 42, 93
Frowick, Robert, 59

G

Georges-Picot, François, 122
Georgievski, Ljubčo, 59
Glenny, Misha, 4
Gligorov, Kiro, 20, 55–58, 108
Goražde rules, 34
Greater Serbia, 5, 9, 46, 120
Greece, 13, 22, 53, 56, 57, 64, 65, 67, 69, 85, 92, 96, 99, 101, 103, 126
Gruevski, Nikola, 57, 62–65, 101, 105
Gulf Cooperation Council, 121

H

Hays, Don, 41
Helsinki Commission of U.S. Congress, 76

Herzeg-Bosna, 36, 39, 40, 44
Holbrooke, Richard, 17, 34, 35, 37, 38, 48, 49, 58
Houthis, 121, 131
Hussein, Saddam, 123, 131

I

Implementation force (IFOR), 26, 40
Interim Accord, 64, 67, 69
International Conference on Yugoslavia, 31
International Court of Justice (ICJ), 64, 69, 85
International Criminal Tribunal for the former Yugoslavia (ICTY), 38, 48, 75, 77
International Organization for Migration, 81
Inzko, Valentin, 42
Iran, 93, 127
Iraq, 14, 21, 22, 48, 116–120, 122, 123, 125–127, 129–131, 133
Irredentism, 56
Ischinger, Wolfgang, 81
Islamic Declaration, 31, 48
Islamic state, 3, 13, 33, 34, 107, 118, 119, 122–129
Islamist extremism, 33
Ivanov, Gjorge, 60, 63
Izetbegović, Alija, 15, 20, 31, 32, 37, 38, 44, 108
Izetbegović, Bakir, 44

J

Josip Broz "Tito", 18, 29, 53

K

Karadžić, Vuk, 19, 36, 74
KFOR, 79, 80, 88, 96
Kosovo, 2–8, 10, 13, 14, 16–18, 20, 21, 24, 30, 54–56, 58, 59, 61, 62, 67, 71–89, 91, 93–112, 116, 117, 120–123, 125, 126, 129, 130, 132
battle of Kosovo Polje, 72
Kosovo Diplomatic Observer Mission, 74
Kosovo Liberation Army (KLA), 18, 73, 74, 80, 102, 106
Kosovo and Metohija, 78
Koštunica, Vojislav, 77, 78
Kotzias, Nikos, 65
Kurdistan, 116, 117, 123, 124, 127, 129, 132
Kurdistan Regional Government (KRG), 123, 124, 131

L

Lajčák, Miroslav, 42
Libya, 23, 24, 118, 120, 127, 128, 131, 132, 134

M

Maastrict Treaty, 31
Macedonia, 1, 3, 4, 6, 7, 9, 10, 13, 14, 16, 20–22, 25, 30, 31, 53–69, 71–73, 82, 86, 91, 92, 94–96, 99, 101, 103, 105, 109, 110, 120, 122, 123, 132
Marković, Ante, 16
Marxism (Marxist), 5
Merkel, Angela, 46, 83, 86
Mihailović, Draža, 9
Millet, 8, 117
Milošević, Slobodan (Milošević), 4, 5, 14, 15, 18, 19, 21, 29–38, 46, 47, 49, 53, 55, 60, 66, 71–79, 87, 88, 95, 101, 102, 108, 116, 118, 129, 130
Montenegro, 3, 7, 9, 10, 16, 20, 22, 30, 77, 78, 84, 86, 91–96, 98, 103, 105, 109
Mother Teresa Society, 73

Mujahideen, 33, 36

N
Name issue, 57, 58, 63–65, 92, 96, 99, 101
National Liberation Army (NLA), 59, 67
NATO, 2, 3, 10, 13, 14, 17, 18, 22, 25, 26, 32–35, 39, 40, 44, 47, 48, 53, 56, 58, 59, 63–66, 69, 71, 74, 75, 79, 80, 83, 84, 87, 91–98, 101, 103, 107–110, 116, 118, 128, 129
Nikolić, Tomislav, 78
North Macedonia, 65, 66
Nouri al-Maliki, 118, 131

O
Obama, Barack, 22, 25, 116
Ohrid Agreement, 6, 59–61, 68
Organization for Security and Cooperation in Europe (OSCE), 24, 59, 61, 74, 80, 81, 88, 120, 121, 128
Otpor!, 76, 77
Ottoman, 8–10, 18, 19, 21, 57, 117
Owen, Roberts, 40
Owen/Stoltenberg, 32

P
Paddy Ashdown, 40
Partition, 3, 21, 33, 34, 36, 59, 118, 121, 123, 125, 126, 132
Partnership for Peace, 63, 96
Petritsch, Wolfgang, 40
Poos, Jacques, 32, 98
Poposki, Nikola, 61
Prespa agreement, 65
Prime Minister Haider al-Abadi, 125

Prlić, Jadranko, 36
Przino agreement, 63, 69
Putin, Vladimir, 80, 94–96, 99, 116, 119, 124, 129, 131

R
Račak, 74
Radicalization, 17, 33
Rambouillet, 18, 74, 76, 91
Regional Cooperation Council, 95, 107, 108, 112
Republika Srpska, 34–40, 42–45, 47, 50, 74, 84, 94, 96, 97, 102, 105, 107
Resolution 1244, 79, 83, 84, 88
Romania, 10, 85, 92, 93, 96, 99, 101, 103, 111, 127
Rugova, Ibrahim, 15, 17, 20, 73, 80, 81, 108
Russia, 3, 4, 18, 21, 23, 24, 47, 66, 71, 79, 85, 94–97, 99, 100, 107, 110, 115, 116, 118, 119, 121, 125, 127–129, 131
Rwanda, 14, 118

S
Sacirbey, Muhamed (Šaćirbegović), 17
Samaras, Antonis, 57, 64, 65
Sanader effect, 64, 100
Schwarz-Schilling, Christian, 42
Serbia, 4, 7–10, 14, 16, 17, 21, 22, 30, 34–37, 40, 44–46, 53–55, 58, 60, 71, 72, 74–79, 81–86, 88, 89, 91, 92, 94–99, 101–103, 105, 108–112, 120, 122, 130, 132
Serbian League of Communists, 72
Serbian question, 19
Šešelj, Vojislav, 74
Silajdžić, Haris, 17, 42
Slovakia, 96, 101

Slovenia, 5, 7, 16, 20, 22, 30, 31, 54, 55, 72, 73, 95, 96, 98, 101, 103, 109
Smith, Chris, 76
Socialist Yugoslavia, 2, 4, 5, 7, 8, 15, 16, 18, 30, 32, 53–55, 61, 92, 121
Soros, George, 76
South Ossetia, 47, 86, 124, 126
Soviet Union, 14, 15, 18, 19, 117, 122, 126
Spain, 101
Srebrenica, 32
Stability Pact, 95, 108, 110
Stabilization and Association Agreement, 84, 100
Stabilization force (SFOR), 40
Standards before status, 81
Standards with status, 82, 84
Sudan, 122
Svilanović, Goran, 107
Syria, 3, 13, 21–24, 33, 48, 94, 115–123, 125–130, 132–134

T
Tadić, Boris, 78
Trump, Donald, 3, 22, 94, 116, 131, 132, 134
Tsipras, Alexis, 65
Tuđman, Franjo (Tuđman), 15, 21, 30, 32–34, 36–38, 108
Turkey, 21, 23, 33, 44, 67, 94, 109, 123, 126–129, 132

U
Ukraine, 3, 10, 13, 21, 23, 24, 47, 94, 96, 97, 99, 100, 115–117, 119–122, 124–132
UNESCO, 81
Unipolar moment, 13, 18, 25, 26, 116
United Arab Emirates, 127
United Nations (UN), 1, 6, 10, 14, 16–19, 24, 26, 32–35, 39, 40, 48, 50, 53, 55, 56, 66, 71, 79–86, 115, 116, 118, 120, 125, 129, 130
United Nations Security Council, 6, 17, 18, 55, 69, 79, 82, 85, 88, 116, 118, 125, 126, 129, 130
UNMIK, 79, 83
UNPREDEP, 55

V
Vance/Owen, 32, 122
Vesna Pusić, 108
Vetëvendosje, 82, 84
Vidovdan, 72
Vojvodina, 30
Vučić, Aleksandar, 78, 79

W
Walker, Bill, 74
Washington Agreement, 6
WHO, 81
Wisner, Frank, 81
World War I, 8, 18, 123
World War II, 2, 9, 18, 30, 53, 126, 132

Y
Yeltsin, Boris, 116
Yemen, 21, 23, 24, 121, 127, 129, 131, 132
Yugoslavia, 5, 7, 10–12, 14–16, 18–20, 24, 25, 29–31, 46–49, 53–55, 67, 72, 77, 79, 86–88, 92, 93, 98, 101, 102, 106, 108, 130, 133

Z
Zaev, Zoran, 62, 63, 65
Zajedno, 76

The manufacturer's authorised representative in the EU is Springer Nature Customer Service Centre GmbH, Europaplatz 3, 69115 Heidelberg, Germany. If you have any concerns regarding our products, please contact ProductSafety@springernature.com

Printed and bound by CPI Group (UK) Ltd, Croydon, CR0 4YY

23/03/2026

02076401-0008